INVEST LIKE A BANK

HOW TO MAKE MILLIONS FROM OTHER PEOPLE'S DEBT. THE BEST 101 GUIDE FOR COMPLETE BEGINNERS TO INVEST IN, BROKER OR FLIP REAL ESTATE DEBT, NOTES, AND DISTRESSED MORTGAGES LIKE A PRO

BEAUX BLAST

WWW.BEAUXBLAST.COM
PUBLISHED BY LUCK AND PROSPERITY PUBLISHING HOUSE

© **Copyright Beaux Blast 2020 - All rights reserved.**

The content contained within this book may not be reproduced, duplicated or transmitted without direct written permission from the author or the publisher.

Under no circumstances will any blame or legal responsibility be held against the publisher, or author, for any damages, reparation, or monetary loss due to the information contained within this book. Either directly or indirectly. You are responsible for your own choices, actions, and results.

Legal Notice:

This book is copyright protected. This book is only for personal use. You cannot amend, distribute, sell, use, quote or paraphrase any part, or the content within this book, without the consent of the author or publisher.

Disclaimer Notice:

Please note the information contained within this document is for educational and entertainment purposes only. All effort has been executed to present accurate, up to date, and reliable, complete information. No warranties of any kind are declared or implied. Readers acknowledge that the author is not engaging in the rendering of legal, financial, medical or professional advice. The content within this book has been derived from various sources. Please consult a licensed professional before attempting any techniques outlined in this book.

By reading this document, the reader agrees that under no circumstances is the author responsible for any losses, direct or indirect, which are incurred as a result of the use of the information contained within this document, including, but not limited to, — errors, omissions, or inaccuracies.

CONTENTS

Acknowledgments   5
Introduction   7

1. The Basics - Everything you Should Know about Mortgage Notes   11
2. Building Your Strategy   34
3. Money Making Math   52
4. The 7 Best Places To Find Notes   83
5. Assembling your Team - Jack of all Trades, Master of None.   117
6. Due Diligence   127
7. The 9 Most Successful Exit Strategies (In Order of Profitability)   158
8. 8. 10x Your Portfolio   178

Conclusion   187
References   191

ACKNOWLEDGMENTS

To everyone I passed on my journey - I couldn't have done it without you. Thanks to my family for all the support you gave me while getting started investing and then while writing this book. This book wouldn't have been finished without your ongoing support.

To the reader, I hope that I can help you as others have helped me. I'm so tired of seeing people give up because they've been misled. I dedicate this book to everyone who tried to get into real estate investing and gave up. I hope this book saves you from giving up and leads you down a path to success that is so strong, nothing will make you turn back.

INTRODUCTION

WHY READ THIS BOOK?

Everyone knows there are only three ways to get rich: Investing, starting a business, or winning the lottery. Since playing the lottery isn't a very great strategy (and only takes 5 minutes anyway), you have plenty of time to focus on the other 2.

If you've been around real estate investors for any length of time, you know that over 90% of millionaires create their wealth by investing in real estate. And while that particular statistic is overused and abused… it's absolutely true.

Since you've picked up this book, I can tell that you've already decided to use real estate to make your millions. Who wouldn't? People will always need a place to live or do business, so it's not going away. And it's proven to be more stable, less risky, and have higher returns in general than the stock market.

Real estate investing is the best way forward. But conventional investing does have problems of it's own. 3 big problems that investors lovingly refer to as "The Three T's".

Termites, toilets and tenants.

The three T's are what make great investors cash out and throw all of their money in the stock market. Even though you won't get as great returns, at least you won't have to wake up at 3 AM to an overflowing toilet, right?

But what if I could teach you how to avoid The Three T's while you invest in real estate? AND you would do it all from the comfort of your own home with a 97% certainty that it was going to be profitable.

Skeptical? Curious?

Good. All the greatest investors are.

I'm going to teach you about the magical world of note investing. An investment strategy so risk-free that even banks do it.

You might not know it yet, but note investing is your ticket to stable, passive income.

Once you have completed this book, you will know how to invest like a bank. You'll discover how to find notes, weigh their value, and choose the most profitable exit strategy.

Be warned - this book is not like other note investing books.

I don't waste precious time telling you about my life, I don't weigh you down with unnecessary information, and I certainly don't waste countless pages on weird testimonials.

No.

This book has one goal: Give you, a complete beginner, all the knowledge you need to invest like a bank in as few pages as possible.

Are you ready to get started?

NOTE INVESTMENT CHECKLIST

(NEVER LEAVE HOME WITHOUT THIS...)

This Checklist will...

- Help you determine if a note is worth your time in 5 minutes
- Be the ONLY Note Intake form you will EVER need
- Is designed to share with other investors for quick turnaround
- **BONUS Checklist: Common Documents needed to assign OR close**!

The last thing we want is for you to get caught with your pants down when someone calls you with a deal. Download this checklist so you always know what to say when a potential lead calls!

To receive your Note Investing Checklist, visit the link:

www.BeauxBlast.com/Debt

THE BASICS - EVERYTHING YOU SHOULD KNOW ABOUT MORTGAGE NOTES

WHAT ARE THEY?

A note is a promise to pay someone back.

So, if you've ever financed a car, used a credit card, or promised to pay your buddy back for the beer he bought last saturday, you have experience with notes.

Ok, maybe that last one is stretching the definition a bit… but you get the point.

As you've probably guessed by now, banks, credit unions, and other financial institutions originate most meaningful notes. But that's not where the story ends. Usually the originator doesn't hang on to the note, especially if it's not performing.

In fact, notes are frequently bought and sold. And, contrary to popular belief, notes are bought by both financial institutions *and* individuals.

This is usually the point when new investors check out. You're probably even more skeptical now because you believe you're going to need hundreds of thousands of dollars to even have a hope of investing in notes.

Good news. You don't.

Notes are frequently bought and sold… *for pennies on the dollar.* And even if you don't have those pennies right now, there's still a very lucrative investment strategy for you that I am going to cover at length later. (Hint, it's called brokering. It costs $0).

So hang tight and keep reading.

WHY NOTES?

I live in the US. If there's one thing I know about this country, it's that people *love* to consume. We get into debt almost as casually as we eat dessert. Americans often want the biggest house, the most luxurious car, or the newest phone - and it's easy for us to get those things, especially if we have no money!

That's great news for note investors because it means *debt is plentiful!*

But what about specifically mortgage debt? After all, we don't want to invest in unsecured debt like credit cards or depreciating assets like cars. We want to invest in loans secured to assets that are likely to appreciate so we can get our money back if the deal falls through *(plus some extra for our troubles).*

Well, good news, mortgage debt in the US is over $10.4 trillion. That's a lot of secured debt on appreciating assets, don't you think?

Not only is there abundant opportunity, investing in notes can be one of the most compassionate ways to invest in real estate.

I grew up watching HGTV. I'm sure a few of you out there did too. From a very young age, I learned that you could flip houses to make money. So, when I joined my first REIA, I thought the only way to invest in real estate was flipping or wholesaling.

I'm sure you've heard of these clubs. They are essentially networking events that also have some information about investing and the local economy. If you go as a new investor and you network your ass off, you might even find an older, more experienced investor to take you under their wing.

That's where I found Tom.

Tom had been investing since 2009. I started talking to him at the local REIAs and eventually, he decided that I was smart and tenacious enough to take me under his wing. In true real estate investor fashion, we had our first meeting at Starbucks.

It was a great meeting. Tom was full of energy and excited to work with me. I was infected with his excitement and ready to start learning from him. I came out of that meeting armed with a foreclosure list and some basic instructions on how to talk to the lucky people on it.

People on the foreclosure list are in a tight spot; they are often one month away from losing their home. It's hard to deal with a major problem like that under normal circumstances, but it's even harder when you have 10 investors harassing you all month. That's right, me and a bunch of other people I didn't really know would call the foreclosure list and try to convince each of them to sell us their home.

As you can imagine, people facing foreclosure who are constantly harassed about it do not react kindly. Instead of being their saviors, we were demons. They each knew that they were screwed and they believed that we were trying to screw them even more.

Meanwhile, as investors, we look at this as a public service.

Afterall, we are helping them save their credit and avoid a foreclosure on their record. Most of us would even offer to let them continue living there as renters - which definitely beats getting kicked out of your house.

But, of course, people going through foreclosure did not see it that way.

Why tell you this story? It's depressing and, even worse, it's off-topic.

I told you this story for one simple reason. We note investors do not have to foreclose upon our borrowers. We have the power to modify their loan.

There are a lot of different ways to invest in mortgage notes, but by far the most fulfilling is to find someone who is about to lose their home and modify their loan so they don't.

When you "become the bank", you have control over the loan. If you come across a non-performing loan (meaning the borrower has missed their payments for 3 consecutive months) you have a choice. You can modify their loan or you can kick them out.

The good news is, these non-performing loans are so cheap that modifying the loan is often the best case scenario for both you and the borrower.

Sounds alright, but if I can do that, why don't banks just save themselves the trouble and modify it themselves?

For starters, financial institutions give these foreclosure cases to case managers. These case managers are not paid based upon how many people they can save from foreclosure - they're paid $20/hour. Even if the case managers did care and wanted to save the families that came across their desk, there's only so much they can do. Banks are strictly regulated and too many bad investments on the books can make them look suspect and force an audit.

So, to simplify... It's often more profitable, more safe, and less trouble overall for financial institutions to foreclose upon their non-performing notes or sell them.

That brings me to another thing I touched on earlier - these loans are secured by the houses that back them! That means, if you can't work something out with the borrower, you can foreclose on them and get the physical house back. So, whatever money you invest is completely secured by the collateral!

MECHANICS OF A NOTE

All notes have the same basic components in their Terms of Agreement.

Payee/Lender/Mortgagor

The entity (a person, a bank or a business) that is lending money. In this case, this is you.

Payor/borrower/Mortgagee

The entity that is borrowing money. In this case, it will more than likely be an individual who wants to own a house.

The Principle

The amount of the loan minus the accumulated interest.

The Interest Rate

The proportion of the loan that is charged as interest to the payee. In this case, we will be using compound interest. The actual rate you are allowed to charge varies by state.

The Number of Payments

This is the number of payments owed. It is also the schedule in which the payor will pay back their loan. You can set this schedule to be whatever you like but generally it is once per month for 15 or 30 years.

The Date

The day the promissory note becomes effective.

Date of First Payment

Not to be confused with The Date above. This is the day that the payor owes you the first payment on their loan.

Date of Final Payment

This is the official date of the final payment on the loan. This date can be calculated by scheduling out the number of payments after the Date of the First Payment.

Late Fee Penalty

This is the penalty the payor will face if they are late for a payment. Usually it is a lump sum of money that starts 10-15 days after the due date for the payment. Each state has different laws that dictate what it can be, but your servicer will take care of all that for you.

Now, when I talk about notes here, I'm only talking about the promise to pay.

A note isn't secured by any collateral on its own. If you were to simply write a note with a homeowner and sign it, you would just own a piece of paper. That is an insecure investment - aka an investment which is not backed by collateral.

Sure, if they stop paying you, you have every right to send collections after them and ruin their credit, but it doesn't mean you will have a legal right to anything they own. So if they don't have the money to pay you, you don't necessarily get all your money back.

This is why we're going to use mortgage notes! Your state may call it a deed-of-trust or a contract. In the note investing space, mortgage is often used as a catch all for any of these terms. The mortgage ties the note to the deed as a lien on the property.

A lien is a general term for the right to keep possession of property belonging to another person until a debt owed by that person is discharged. A mortgage is a type of lien. Sometimes, you'll even hear people say "mortgage lien".

The third and last component is the deed. A deed is a document which asserts ownership of a property. I'm sure you've seen the old cartoons where some crook steals the deed to a mansion and claims that it belongs to him now it... well, the legal process of transferring a deed is a little more complicated, but yeah, that's pretty much what I'm talking about.

So we have our three components here, the note, the mortgage lien, and the deed. We know that our note is a secured investment because the mortgage asserts that if the borrower fails to pay for a certain time, we will foreclose on them and use their property as collateral.

WHERE ARE THESE NOTES?

After a note has been originated, it can be sold at the sole discretion of the note holder. The place these notes are sold is called the secondary market.

Both financial institutions and individual investors sell notes on the secondary market for a variety of reasons. Maybe they have a performing note but need a lump sum now. Maybe the note is not performing and they don't want to deal with non-performing notes. Maybe they flipped a non-performing note and it's re-performing.

I have an entire chapter dedicated to telling you where to find all kinds of notes. The long and short of it is: finding notes is a delicate balance between networking and marketing with financial institutions, real estate professionals, and other investors.

There are a variety of ways you can find notes - calling banks, looking at wholesale sites, or even networking on LinkedIn. I will go over the 7 best ways to find them in chapter 4, so stay tuned.

HOW DOES NOTE INVESTING WORK?

Now that you know what a note is, I can give you an overview of how we use them to make money. I'm not going to

THE BASICS - EVERYTHING YOU SHOULD KNOW AB... | 21

stand here and say that note investing is easy - like most worthwhile investments, it's not at first. It takes hard work, dedication, and mental fortitude.

However, I happen to believe that the average human has all of those qualities. So, if you want to be an average human that makes above average returns, note investing is the way to do it.

Let's start out with a few categories that investors use to distinguish notes: performing v non-performing, first-lien v second-lien, and commercial v residential.

Because investing in notes is such a rich field to get into, you really just want to pick one type and go all in. If you don't, you'll probably get overwhelmed. But don't worry, there's a strategy for everyone and I help you find yours in chapter 2.

Once you've found a note that you want to invest in, you perform due diligence. I like to do my due diligence in 2 steps - a cursory glance and a deep dive. Due diligence will tell you how much you will get for the note, what kind of note it is, and if it's a good investment overall. More on that in chapter 6.

Once you've found a note that you would like to purchase, you negotiate for it. After you've negotiated your loan, you will either start collecting cash (performing) or you will fix the note and then collect cash (Non-performing).

It takes 3 things to be successful in this business - knowledge (which you are well on your way to gaining by reading this book), relationships (which I will show you how to cultivate), and either time OR money. Having both time and money is great but you really just need one of them to succeed.

Note investing has a high barrier to entry. But I think you'll find that flipping a note is a lot easier than flipping a house. And keeping a note for the long term is a lot easier than having tenants.

TAXES

Investing in Notes can be very tricky, so I hope you take my advice and hire an accountant.

But I'd be remiss if I didn't at least give you some information about taxes on notes.

Any income you generate from a note is taxable income that needs to be reported. The income is the interest you earned from that note for that particular tax year. That means, any payment towards the principle is not taxable, but the interest you make on those payments is. Exactly how much you will be taxed depends on your tax bracket, which type of business you open, and the craftiness of your accountant.

I am not an accountant, nor do I play one on TV, so make sure you consult with an accountant come tax season.

ORIGINATION

There are 3 main ways that notes are originated. Institutional, Seller-financed, and Non-bank lending notes.

Institutional

Institutionally originated mortgages are originated through financial institutions. These notes are generally worth more and supposedly safer to invest in. Banks usually have a more rigorous review process than a random homeowner.

Banks also often sell their non-performing notes all at once in the form of "a tape". One strategy we will talk about at length is buying a tape, keeping the notes you really like and selling the rest. This is one way to invest in notes when you have no money and is referred to as brokering.

Seller-Financed

Seller financed mortgages are mortgages that are originated from an individual. So, if you owned a house outright and decided to sell it, you could theoretically owner finance it out. That means the new owners would pay you like they would pay a bank - interest and everything.

Yep! That's one way for you to "become the bank"!

Originating your own mortgage notes is definitely a strategy you should explore, but it is not one we will go over in this book. But, buying them after they have already been financed is the topic of this book. The tl;dr is seller financed notes are pretty similar to institutionally financed notes - your title company will probably just find more mistakes.

Non-bank Lending Notes

Non-bank lending notes are not often talked about in the note space because they are rare and often short-lived.

These notes are primarily originated from hard money lenders. If you've never heard of hard money lending before, they usually work with flippers. They will finance the entire deal - from the cost of the house to the cost of the materials and labor.

This usually results in a note that has a very high interest rate but only lasts for a year or two. Because of how short lived these loans are, the hard money lender will probably lose money if they have to sell them.

So, they're pretty rare, but you may run across them.

COMMON PAYMENT STRUCTURES

Fixed-Rate

This is where the interest rate does not change for the duration of the entire mortgage. Of course, if you refinance, the rate can change. But the bank can't just change your interest rate willy nilly.

Floating Rate

This is also referred to as an adjustable mortgage rate(ARMs). ARMs are when the rate changes based on a previously agreed upon index such as Libor, cost of funds index(COFI) or the monthly treasury average (MTA). Usually, the rate follows these indexes but adds a margin. For example, if you take out a 2% margin based on COFI and COFI is at 5%, then the mortgage's rate will adjust up to 7%.

ARMS have a couple pros: first, they tend to have lower introductory rates than fixed mortgages. That means you're initially charged less interest. The rates can also float down when the index fund floats down. However, the negative to this is that it can go up as well. So, if the index you are tracking goes up, so does your interest for that period.

Fixed/Floating

Commercial loans are generally structured this way. For the first xx years, the rate is fixed, but then it behaves like an ARM.

Balloon

This is where the principal is due at the end of the balloon period, but the borrower pays as if they are paying for a longer term.

For instance, let's say you have a loan that has a 10-year term but is amortized over a 30-year period. What that means is you pay principle and interest as if the mortgage was going to last 30 years, but after 10 years you pay the remainder of your balance.

Don't worry - you'll know all about this by the time you've finished reading chapter 3, which is all about math.

Interest-Only Mortgage Note

The principle is not amortized, it is due in full at maturity. For the duration of the loan, the borrower only needs to make interest payments. They can always pay more, but they are only on the hook for the interest owed each month. At the end of the term, the borrower pays the remaining balance on the mortgage.

Negative Amortization Mortgage Note

This loan can cost the borrower more in the long run because they can pay less than the interest charged each month. Any extra, unpaid interest is added to the principal. This makes the principal amount increase and thus increases the amount of interest charged.

Out of all of these strategies, Fixed-rate loans are the safest for a risk-averse investor because there is less chance that the payor will default at any point on the loan. You can utilize any of these strategies, but make sure the strategy fits the borrower.

If your borrower is an investor, they probably understand how balloons work and are smart enough to refinance before it pops. If it's someone who could barely afford a mortgage and has a low credit score, you probably want to stick with the safer bet.

KNOWLEDGE

This book is intended to be a launching platform. There is no way that I can fit everything you need to know about note investing into a single book - this niche is way too big! There are way too many scenarios, deal structures, and different types of notes to fit everything you need to know into a single book or course.

That said, this book tells you exactly what you need to

know to get started and helps you form a plan to succeed with the least amount of risk possible. Once you've read this book, you'll know 80% of what you need to know. You'll learn the last 20 through good old experience. You have to.

They say it takes 10,000 hours to master anything. I don't really think that's true, but let's say it is. You probably want to be successful way before 10,000 hours in. Who wouldn't?

I have some great news. You don't have to wait 10,000 hours to buy and sell your first note. In fact, I bet success finds you before 100 hours. But you need to spend your time wisely. Picking up this book was a great first step - it will probably take you 4 hours to read and digest. What do you do after this book?

In order to be successful, you need to pick a direction and stick with it. Decide which notes you want to invest in and follow the directions I outline in this book. Go all in for 10 hours a week for 10 weeks. It's not a trivial amount of time, but I bet you can carve that out of your week if you try hard enough.

Go on youtube and watch other successful note investors. Read the news about notes. Find some online note investing meetings. Do everything you can to learn for the first 20 hours. Then, start applying your knowledge by using one of the strategies in chapter 4.

We live in a wonderful time where finding mentors is easy. My opinion on mentors is this - spend at least 100 hours learning about something before you hire someone to help you. Usually, if you learn for 100 hours and talk about it with other interested parties, you can find a mentor for free.

And if you can't?

Once you know the basics and the language of note investing, you will be able to pick out the scammers. Don't let yourself get picked up by a fraud - learn how to invest in notes before you buy an expensive course.

RELATIONSHIPS

If knowledge is the main course then relationships are the secret sauce. You can buy some notes without forming relationships, but it will only get you so far. Eventually, you will want to 10x your business. If you want to find super discounted notes, have an "unlimited" pool of money, and make safe investments, relationships are key.

There are three main types of relationships - people who sell, people who buy, and people who give you money to invest.

Simple? Good.

That leaves you three groups of people - other investors, regular people, and banks. Other investors will often buy, sell and invest in your business. Regular people don't invest in notes, but they trust you to turn a profit for them and give you their money in hopes that that is what you do. As for banks, most of them will only sell you notes.

So, where do you find these relationships?

INVESTOR RELATIONSHIPS

There are quite a few places to find other investors. For starters, you can go on Bigger Pockets and make a post. "Any other note investors out there?". You can also search for previous posts about note investing and contact each of those investors. Some of them are trying to sell products and others are just going to have more experience. Remember, don't buy anything until you kind of know what you're doing.

The next best place - FaceBook groups and LinkedIn groups! Go on FaceBook and LinkedIn, and type in "Note Investing" in the search bar. You'll get about 10 groups. Sure, some of them will be closed, but some of them are open. Join all of the open groups! For the first few months, do not post anything, just read. Soak it up. Remember, 100 hours!

When you do find your first deal, these online forums are going to be your best friend. You can ask detailed questions and get kind, detailed responses. It's almost like having 100 mentors by your side.

The next place you're going to meet people is your local REI group. Go to meetup.com and type in Real Estate Investing. You might find 1, maybe you'll find 10. It depends on your city.

Go to those meetings for a few months and make yourself visible. Trade contact information, offer to take them to lunch, and pay attention to what everyone is looking for. This is a great place to find people who are doing local deals. It's well worth the $20 of admission.

The last place you can find other investors is conferences. There are tons of conferences that happen every year for note investing. Usually they cost under $1000. Does that seem like a lot to you? If you really don't have the money to go, stick to the free options I mentioned. But if you want to jump in head first, go to a conference. They are seriously amazing. Everyone there is a note investor looking to network. Collect business cards, add people into your CRM and use this to catapult your network forward.

Normal People

Normal people are anyone you know. Really.

We'll talk about this later in the book but you will run out of money eventually. One of the strategies note investors use is to ask other investors, friends, family, and acquaintances if they would like to make an xx profit.

Some gurus suggest you ask them before you have a solid deal. I don't. I don't feel like it's right for an unproven investor to start collecting money from their family and friends. If you fail, not only are you in debt, you're also at risk of destroying relationships.

Once you have done a few deals, you can start mentioning your new business prospect to your family, friends, and acquaintances. Don't try to collect money from anyone until you know what you're doing.

Banks

Forming a relationship with a bank is the same as forming a relationship with anyone else. We will talk about it at length later, but you really want to focus on the people behind the bank, not the institution itself. It's a complicated question with a very long winded answer. So hang tight!

Action

Relationships and knowledge are very important... but none of it matters without action. If you don't take action, you'll never get anywhere. Rarely does anything valuable fall into anyone's lap - so if you're waiting for the universe to gift you a great opportunity... well I have news for you.

You're wasting your time.

Some of you out there also probably don't want to take action. People make a lot of excuses for themselves: Maybe you understand that making your dreams come true takes a lot of work. Maybe you're scared of screwing something up. Maybe you feel like you need to know EVERYTHING before you do ANYTHING.

Get those thoughts out of your head right now. You don't need to know everything. You don't need to be perfect. And you're going to have to work your ass off. After 20 hours of learning, do *something*. It doesn't matter what, just get yourself out there and take some action.

Do not use learning as an excuse to never take action!

That said, let's dive in!

2

BUILDING YOUR STRATEGY

There are a million strategies you can use to make money with notes but not all of them will work for you. You need to find the strategies that line up with your personality, wallet and unique situation.

First, there are a few questions that you need to ask yourself. I'd advise writing down your answers and being as specific as possible. Make sure you know exactly how much time and money you will be investing each week and be very clear about your goals. It will help you decide which type of note to try to specialize in first.

Question	Answer
How much time do you have each week to invest in notes?	
How much money do you have to invest in notes?	
Are you looking for cash-flow or large lump sums?	
Are you doing this because you want to own the collateral?	
Will you be raising private money?	
How much risk are you willing to take on?	
Do you have special knowledge of a certain asset type, process, or location?	

WHICH TYPE OF NOTE IS RIGHT FOR ME?

Notes are usually described using the following three categories:

1. Performing vs Non-Performing
2. Residential vs Commercial
3. Lien Position

PERFORMING VS NON-PERFORMING

Performing Notes

Performing notes are basically when the borrower has been making their payments ontime. Usually, they are seasoned, which means the payments have been on time for at least a year. Even better if it's been 2 years.

Statistically, only 3% of people default on their loan and more than half of them do it within their first 2 years, so if the note has been seasoned and is still performing, you are more than likely never going to have a problem. Sure, random things do happen, people get sick, lose their jobs, etc but for the most part this is as close to risk-free, passive income as it gets.

Performing notes will give you the least amount of return because they are also the least risky and the most valued. You will not see the crazy 3 cent prices for performing notes because they are almost guaranteed to pay out with no further effort on your part.

So, as you've probably guessed, they're more expensive because they are less risky and require less of your time. If you have no time, don't want to hire a team, and just want some easy cash-flow, this is a great place to start. In fact, if you have the money, I would suggest your first note is a performing note.

You might be wondering why anyone would sell a performing note.

To answer your question with another question, why does anyone sell any investment?

They need the cash.

Just like your borrower, random things can happen in the seller's life too. It could be bad or it could be good. Maybe they got sick… or maybe they've found a better investment. Part of due diligence is discovering why they are selling. It could help you avoid trouble and negotiate a better deal.

You can find some performing notes with great returns, but it isn't going to be as great as a non-performing. I can't give you a figure because each situation is different but I can tell you they probably won't be the mind boggling 50% returns you see from non-performing notes. That means that if you have more time than money, performing notes may not be a great way to go. If you've only got $4000 but you've got all the time in the world, you probably want to look into our next topic, non-performing notes!

Normally, banks do not sell performing notes, so you'll either have to network with other investors or use an aggregation site for these guys. Don't worry, we go over this in more detail in chapter 4.

Non-Performing Notes

They say when you buy a performing note, you're buying an investment but when you buy a non-performing note, you're buying a job. Why would anyone want to buy non-performing notes? Isn't the point to passively invest?

The answer? Non-performing notes are like houses that need to be flipped. Sure, they might need some work in order to fix them up, but once you do, you're going to make amazing returns.

You might be wondering exactly how much work non-performing notes are. I'm not going to sit here and tell you that they are easy to flip - because it takes a lot of talking, negotiating, and math to figure out how to make them profitable… but I will say that you are not the one doing all the work.

Foreclosure? You've got a guy for that.

Checking the title? You've got a guy for that.

Running comps? Yep, you've got a guy for that.

Seriously, you just have to figure out which notes are profitable and how to make money from them. Once you do that, your team takes care of the details. Of course you can choose to take care of the details by yourself, but hiring an expert to take care of it is well worth the money.

If you're wondering how much your team will cost, I have good news. You probably don't need a team at all for your first few notes because I recommend you *broker* them. Brokering is basically when you find a profitable note and then you sell it to an investor for a little more than you bought it for.

Say you find a non-performing note for 35 cents (on the dollar) and you find an investor who is willing to pay 37 cents. You get to keep the 2 cents spread! Brokering is not a great strategy for long term, passive income but when you're first starting out, aside from buying a performing note, brokering non-performing notes is the best way to learn.

Even if you do have money, you should still broker your first few non-performing notes. It's free education.

Think about it, if you can't find someone to buy it, then it's probably a bad deal. And besides, you don't know how much anything is worth when you first start out anyway. If you have a lot of other investors turning up their noses, then you know you're about to make a mistake and buy a note for too much. You either renegotiate or back out. Either way, you lose no money.

Non-performing notes are great if you want to own the collateral in the end. Buying the note is often much cheaper than buying the property. And, once you have the non-performing note, you can either convince or force the borrower to sell their house. More on that in chapter 7.

Non-performing notes seem more risky than performing

notes because you aren't getting a guaranteed cash-flow right off the bat, but if you do good due diligence (not perfect, just good) then the risks aren't that high. Remember, if they stop paying, their note is backed by their collateral so you can always repossess their collateral and sell it again.

There are only so many things that can go wrong with a note, so as long as you do your due diligence, you can mitigate a lot of the risk of non-performing notes. Keep in mind that this is a data driven business. You can know 85% of what you need to know just from looking at the data. That's more than most people know when they invest in the stock market!

Category	Rating for Performing Notes	Rating for Non-performing Notes	Explanation
Time	💵💵	💵💵💵	Performing notes need to be sourced from individuals across many different mediums. Non-performing notes can be sourced by banks but also need to be flipped.
Cost	💵💵💵💵	💵💵	
Returns	💵💵	💵💵💵💵💵	
Likelihood of owning the collateral	💵	💵💵💵	With non-performing notes, if you want to own the collateral, it is very easy to own the collateral. There is no chance of owning the collateral of a performing note unless the borrower becomes delinquent (stops paying).
Risk	💵	💵💵💵	If you are unlucky enough to have to foreclose on a non-performing note, it could take you a year or longer. Don't worry, there are a few strategies you can use to avoid this in every case but the worst case.
Special Knowledge Needed?	💵	💵💵	If you plan on hiring a team, you will need basic knowledge, but not a lot.

RESIDENTIAL VS COMMERCIAL

Residential Notes

Residential notes use a house as collateral. These notes are not limited to the mortgage. They can also be a second mortgage to pay for a pool, kitchen, solar panels, etc or a HELOC. Any residential note can be performing or non-performing and reside in any lien position.

We will spend most of this book talking about residential notes. They are the notes a beginner should start with because they are not as expensive and are not as tricky as commercial notes. Remember, you might own whatever your note is tied to - everyone can rent out or sell a house. Not everyone can run a gas station (An example of a commercial note).

Commercial Notes

Commercial notes are notes that back commercial property. Companies can also leverage debt to purchase real estate. Multifamily, construction, and commercial property loans are the three main categories of commercial notes. Within those categories, there are even further specializations like gas stations, hotels, and shopping centers.

Multifamily is a mortgage made on 5 or more units. These units can be either residential or mixed-use.

Construction loans are taken out to start on construction. It can be for houses, land, or commercial development.

Commercial property loans can be for either owner-occupied or non-owner occupied buildings. That means the borrower either houses their business in their property or they are renting it to another business.

You can invest in either performing or non-performing loans. Performing notes are very profitable in the Commercial Note investing world! You can usually purchase these loans for 50%-80% Loan-to-value (LTV) and the interest is higher than what you could get from a standard residential note. The commercial foreclosure process also offers you extra protections because you "have recourse if you aren't made whole". That's a fancy way of saying the borrower owes you what you have left on your investment if you foreclose and do not make back what you invested.

If you want to invest in any kind of commercial note, you will need to have at least a couple hundred thousand dollars. It doesn't have to be your money, but generally you need to prove you know what you're doing before people will invest with you. So unfortunately, residential is probably the best place to get your feet wet if you aren't already a millionaire.

Non-performing commercial notes give you an entirely new set of opportunities and challenges. Not only are notes considered non-performing when the owner defaults, they are also non-performing when there are changes in collateral value, bad acts by the borrowers, misplaced insurance paperwork, balloon loans that have matured and have not been refinanced, property transfers, and past-due property taxes.

Recourse sounds pretty good! As does that purchase price. But, don't start daydreaming about owning a note for an office building yet - there are a few risks.

The biggest risk involves environmental issues. If you buy a property that has environmental issues, you are responsible for them. That means the government will hold you accountable for either cleaning it or paying the fine. Be careful when you invest in vacant land, gas stations, and other commercial buildings that could have damaged the environment.

The next risk is if the borrower chooses to file for bankruptcy - which can take years to work its way through the courts. If you are about to purchase a note, you need to be sure the borrower is not about to file for bankruptcy - it really decreases the value of your note.

Last but not least is the risk from the ever-changing landscape of the market. If the market changes enough from the beginning of your investment to the end of your exit strategy, you could make much less than you had previously anticipated.

Investing in commercial real estate really comes down to how much risk you are willing to take on. If you can take on extreme risk, then non-performing commercial notes might be the place to go, but I would still recommend you start by brokering these notes. It's a lower barrier to entry and you won't get stuck with a commercial property you have no idea what to do with that has broken several environmental regulations.

Category	Rating for Residential	Rating for Commercial	Explanation
Time	🗎🗎🗎	🗎🗎🗎	The amount of time is dependent upon if they are performing or non-performing
Cost	🗎🗎	🗎🗎🗎🗎	Houses cost less than commercial buildings in raw cash. However, it is technically "cheaper" to purchase commercial notes when you look at what you'll pay for them vs the LTV.
Returns	🗎🗎	🗎🗎🗎🗎	
Likelihood of owning the collateral	🗎🗎🗎	🗎🗎🗎	Owning the collateral is highly dependent on if they are non-performing notes.
Risk	🗎🗎🗎	🗎🗎	If you foreclose on your commercial note, it will be faster and you have the option of recourse. Residential foreclosures take a long time and do not have the same guarantee.
Special Knowledge Needed?	🗎	🗎🗎🗎🗎	You need to be prepared to own any commercial building you invest in.

LIEN POSITION

There can quite literally be an infinite amount of liens attached to a property. However, I have never seen more than 5.

As a note investor, you are mostly interested in either the first or the second lien. In some cases, investors are interested in purchasing the third lien, but that is more like playing the lottery and less like investing.

I caution you to stay away from any lien beyond the second lien because they are not worth that much. You'll be shocked at how little people will want to pay for them. So start out with first and second until you know what you're doing and then, if you're feeling lucky, you can move into third+.

In most cases, liens are *usually* positioned in the order they were written. Let me explain: Say you buy a house. You put down your 20% downpayment and use a bank to originate your mortgage. Your mortgage is the first position lien.

Now, let's say 10 years go by. You and your wife still live there and now you've even had a few kids. One day, someone knocks on your door to sell you solar panels. You're pretty excited about this because you like the idea of never paying for electricity again. So, you put down 10% of the price of the solar panels.

The solar panel company will put a second lien on your home for the remaining balance of the solar panels.

Why is it a second lien?

Because it was attached to your property second.

But why should you care which position a note investment is?

First- and second-lien notes are both originated from the same documents and bestow the same legal right to collect. That means that you can start foreclosure on the home from any position if the borrower is delinquent on your lien. However, the first lien will collect their portion first. The lien position is also the priority in which the note will be paid off when the home is foreclosed on.

A first position note is the most secure because it is paid off first. The second position is only paid if the first position is fully paid. If you do not have enough left over from the auction to pay the second position, it just drops off (in the case of residential investing).

Let's go back to the previous example. Imagine you lost your job 2 months after the solar panels were installed. Since your wife stays home with the kids, your job was the only income and now you can't pay your mortgage. Eventually, your home goes through foreclosure. The bank takes control of your house and sells it for less than you owe them. The bank would get all the money and the solar panel company would get nothing.

The good news is that you don't owe either of them any money because foreclosure wipes out all liens. The bad news is your credit score is now in the garbage and you have a foreclosure on your record for the next 7 years.

Much like depending on a 9 to 5 job instead of having multiple streams of income, being in a second lien position is more dangerous than in a first lien position. The debt owed to you could be completely wiped out and you'd have little control over it. Even if the solar panel company had foreclosed upon the house, the bank who originated their mortgage would still be paid first. Of course, the solar panel company could gain possession of the property and assume the first position lien, but that is a topic for another time.

That is, in general, how liens work. However, like most legal processes, there are exceptions for the government. If the borrower stops paying their property taxes, the government will attach a lien to the home. The government gets the first position, no matter what. Depending on what state you are investing in, the property can then be sold at a tax auction… which effectively wipes away any other debt exactly like a foreclosure.

Usually, if there are overages from the tax sale, the first position lien can collect them... but that doesn't mean it's enough to cover your costs. It's the same with municipality liens and some HOA liens. They cut to the front of the line of existing liens.

There are other types of liens - IRS liens, Medical liens, mechanical liens etc, but those will usually follow the borrower around if there is a foreclosure, so you don't necessarily have to worry about those.

A little confused?

That's ok, all that matters for now is you know, in general, how liens work. Each situation is different, so if you find these liens on your note, you just need to talk to your lawyer about which ones fall off and which ones stay on. It will vary by state, which is why I will not go too much into detail here.

Despite all of the above, first Lien mortgages seem like the obvious choice, right? It's much more secure than the second lien. I mean, at least you've got a higher chance of getting paid if the borrower decides to default, right?

Exactly.

So, that means you will always pay more for a first position than you would for a second position.

BUILDING YOUR STRATEGY | 49

If you want to purchase second-position liens, it's less risky to purchase one that has some equity and is following a performant first-position lien. Sometimes, people don't realize that a second-position lien can foreclose upon them, so you can usually fix it by sending them a letter threatening to do so.

If you want to get the cheapest notes possible, you can also try your hand with a delinquent first lien and a second lien with negative equity. Negative equity means the borrower owes more than what the collateral is worth. I would not suggest purchasing these non-performing second lien notes because the return rates are absolutely abysmal.

You might buy 100 of them, but only 3 would be profitable! It can be very discouraging for a new investor, so I'd recommend first position, non-performing or second position non-performing with a performing first-position.

Category	Rating for 1st position	Rating for 2nd position	Explanation
Time	🗒🗒🗒	🗒🗒🗒	The amount of time is dependent upon if they are performing or non-performing
Cost	🗒🗒🗒🗒	🗒🗒	
Returns	🗒🗒🗒	🗒🗒	
Likelihood of owning the collateral	🗒🗒🗒	🗒🗒	
Risk	🗒	🗒🗒🗒	
Special Knowledge Needed?	🗒	🗒🗒	When investing in second-position liens, you need to know more about how liens work in order to find clever ways to make money.

YOUR GOALS

Now that you know a little more about what you will be investing in, it's time to think about your goals. After you've brokered a few notes, you will have the knowledge and resources you need to start actually investing in them.

Note investing is a very deep niche and while you should definitely be aware of the different types of notes, I would advise you pick one to specialize in.

You can use the information from this chapter to select the type of note that you think you would like to invest in. Keep those notes in mind as you continue to read this book.

That said, if you want to specialize in non-performing notes, commercial notes, or third+ lien notes, you should start by either investing in performing notes or brokering note. Here is the general strategy you should follow before you start investing in the riskier investments.

1. (If you have money) Invest in some 1st or 2nd position, residential performing notes. This will be the least amount of risk and can be found on some aggregation sites I share in chapter 4. You can also find these by advertising your services to other investors. If you have the money to invest in these notes, it gives you a quick win and great returns.

You will also understand how all the paperwork works and the overall process of investing.

2. (Switch this step with step 1 if you have no money) Broker some 1st or 2nd position non-performing notes. They don't have to be residential, they can be commercial because you are selling them to other investors. I will show you how to find these notes in chapter 4. Brokering is a great first step if you have no money because it won't cost you anything and will actually net you income. However, finding notes to broker will take a while so it will not be a quick win.
3. Once you have brokered some notes, visit step 1 and purchase some performing notes.
4. Start investing in the type of note you would like to specialize in and broker the rest of them. You'll come across all types of notes in your time as a note investor. You won't be knowledgeable about all of them. Broker the notes you don't want to keep. Keep the notes that you specialize in.

** Note Icon made by Pixel perfect from www.flaticon.com

3

MONEY MAKING MATH

When you find a deal, how do you know it's a good one?

Note due diligence involves a lot of math.

You might want to figure out what your investment will be worth in the future, how much of the note you need to sell to make up for a down payment, how much will be left on a balloon when it pops, etc etc.

I separated learning the math from the due diligence process because you need to understand the calculations before you know how to use them. Thankfully, all you really need to understand is what each type of formula does because most of the math is handled for you by a financial calculator.

MONEY MAKING MATH | 53

With that in mind, let's talk about 2 of the most important concepts of investing: *Time Value of Money(TVM)* and *risk vs return.*

TIME VALUE OF MONEY

The concept of the time value of money is very simple: today's dollar is worth less than tomorrow's.

If you let your money sit in a checking account, you will have less spending power next year - even if you have exactly the same amount of money. Obviously, this is the opposite of what we want. We want to have more spending power in our bank account than last year so we can live on it indefinitely. That's the whole point of investing.

If you want proof of this, ask someone that bought a house in 1990 how much they paid. I asked a few of my older relatives what they paid for their homes back in the day. In the 70's, I had answers like $20,000 for a 2 bed 3 bath! In the 90's, it was $50,000.

Riddle me this. Why does the same house in the same city cost $150,000 this year?

If you said inflation, you're right on the money.

When you invest, you should aim to make returns greater

than the cost of inflation. In the US, inflation is about 2.5%. That means your money loses, on average, 2.5% of its spending power each year.

If investing was a war, inflation would be your enemy.

But, there is a weapon you can use to combat inflation: interest.

There are 2 main types of interest - *compound interest* and *simple interest.*

Simple interest is calculated using the current principle of the loan.

Compound interest is calculated using the principle as well as the accumulated interest of previous periods. You may have heard compound interest referred to as interest on interest because the interest will also earn interest.

Using compound interest instead of simple interest makes a huge difference for your returns over time, especially when you have a high interest rate. That's why most mortgages are structured using compound interest.

Now that we know about interest and inflation, we need to talk about opportunity cost. Opportunity cost is considering the tradeoffs of one opportunity vs another.

We all do this every day, whether we realize it or not. Choosing between going to a party and staying home involves considering the opportunity cost just as much as considering which note you're going to buy involves an opportunity cost.

When considering notes, you need to think about a few things - mainly the profit vs the amount of time you'll spend on it. For instance, maybe you have 2 opportunities on your desk - one of them is a performing notes with a 12% yield, but it costs $20,000. The other is 2 non-performing notes that each have the potential to give you a 20% return for the same price.

Take a second and think about the opportunity cost here.

The performing note has guaranteed returns and will use up almost none of your time. However, the returns are not as great as the non-performing note (npn). The npn would give you excellent returns but would require a lot of work.

You might have thought *the npn also has a risk! What if it takes 2 years to foreclose!*

I'm glad you asked because that brings us to our next topic.

RISK VS RETURN

Every investment can be placed on a spectrum of risk vs reward. Every investor has a different level of risk they are willing to take. Some investors are willing to risk everything if the reward is tantalizing enough while others are only willing to take small risks. If you completed chapter 2, you should know, roughly speaking, where on the spectrum you are.

Fortunately for you, the way I suggest you go about note investing does not involve a crazy amount of risk. If you follow the advice I give you in this book, you will have a 95% certainty of your yield from any deal. The other 5% will account for all of the random things that *might* happen along the way.

Let's face it, you can't really tell the future. Anything that involves another person is subject to random happenstance. Your borrower could lose a job, get very sick, or go to jail. You can't be 100% sure. We can mitigate the risks by checking job history, credit scores, setting our LTV so that we can deal with disaster scenarios etc but we cannot be 100% sure of the future. People are just too random.

FUTURE VALUE OF MONEY

Note investing is made up of 2 basic concepts. The first is the future value of money: how much is your dollar going to be worth at some point in the future. Fortunately, this concept can be stated in the form of an equation: $(1+1)^N$.

This equation uses interest(I) to calculate what your dollar will be worth in N years.

Disclaimer: If you're scared of math, don't worry. After I am done explaining these concepts, I will introduce you to a calculator that does most of the math for you.

But first, let's do an example to demonstrate how the future value of money works. Take $1 and compound it by 10% over a period of time.

$(1 + 1)^{10} = 1.10$

After 1 year, your dollar would be worth $1.10. What will it be worth after 2 years?

$(1.1 + 1)^{10} = 1.21$

Your dollar would be worth $1.21 because we are performing the calculation on the new value of $1.10. Pretty neat considering you didn't have to do anything at all to make 21 cents.

As you can see, the more money you have, the more it will grow. So, as the years go by, your money will compound upon itself. In a thousand years, 1 dollar can turn into a million with even a modest interest rate.

Let's say you have a job that only pays you exactly what you need to live and leaves you little time to do any other work. You feel like life is hopeless until one day, a distant relative dies and leaves you $50,000.

You manage to get a hold of this book and decide to invest in notes. You realize that you would rather invest the money now in hopes of one day retiring early. *Afterall* you reason *I'm living just fine right now.*

Of course, all your friends laugh at you. They think you need to go on vacation and blow that money like a normal person. But, you're not a normal person - you're a smart guy that trusts his instincts and your instincts are shouting at you to invest the money.

So, you take that $50,000 and invest in 10 non-performing notes. You get an average ROI of 18%! Instead of taking any of that money out, you just invest it in more notes as they come to term. After 30 years, how much would you make from that original $50,000?

$7,168,531.

Seven. Million dollars.

How were we able to calculate that? With the future value of money equation! Give it a try.

PRESENT VALUE OF MONEY

The second concept is how to calculate what today's money is worth from a future amount. If you memorized the future formula, this one will be easy to remember because it's just the inverse.

$1/(1+1)^N$

The present value is useful for calculating the discount of future money to today's dollars. I know it's kind of hard to think about because people don't normally think in those terms so I'll introduce another tool that will help - the *rule of 72*.

The rule of 72 is simple. Divide 72 by the interest rate to see how long it will take your money to double.

Let's say the only way you will forgo the opportunity to purchase a brand new car is if the money you would pay for the car (For the sake of this example, we'll just say it's $50,000) doubles in 3 years. What interest rate do you need for it to double? Take 72/3 and you will see that it takes 24% interest to double (the original interest rate from the future).

This brings us to one of the fundamental rules of investing. You want to borrow money for as long as possible BUT you want to collect as quickly as possible.

Think about it…

If you take a loan from your father at $1000 today for 0% interest to invest in a note, you could make a lot of money at no cost to yourself. Let's say he's willing to wait 30 years for that $1000. Well, if you invest it at an 18% interest rate, it's going to be worth $143,370.

Even if your father charged you 10% interest over 30 years and you had to pay him back $17,449, you'd still be making well over $100,000! The difference between your yield and your payback amount is the spread. Using a spread to make money is the ultimate leveraging tactic and the reason that so many poor people become rich from real estate. They learn how to turn $0 into a million by understanding the present value vs the future value and investing in the spread.

A NOTE ON YIELD VS INTEREST

A quick note here - when we invest in notes, we are investing in discounted notes. So, the interest rates will probably not be 24%. We aren't investing in unsecured credit card debt, we're investing in mortgages. The notes you invest in will probably have an interest rate around 5% or maybe even 10%.

However, since you will be buying them at a steep discount (remember, pennies on the dollar!) your *yield* can be 24%. The yield is income earned on an investment, often expressed as a percentage.

Yield and interest can be the same. For instance, if you were originating the note, then your interest would be your yield, but since we're buying them at a discount, it is a little more complicated.

THE 10BII CALCULATOR

You can try to do all of the following calculations on a regular calculator if you're exceptional at math and love headaches.

However, if you're a normal guy like me, you'd better get a financial calculator.

There are a few different financial calculators, but I'm going to use the 10bII (pronounced 10-b-2). It's what I learned on, and you know what they say about old dogs learning new tricks.

Besides, it's only 6 bucks on the app store and those 6 dollars are well worth the pain it will save you. If you prefer a physical calculator, you can get one at calc.beauxblast.com.

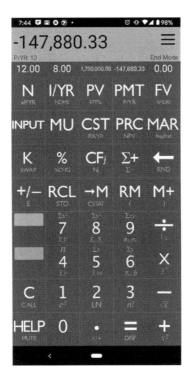

10B11 Calculator

As for using the calculator, you will see a number pad, some buttons with letters, and a red and blue button on the lower left side. The red and blue buttons are called the shift buttons. If you look closely under the white letter and number buttons, you'll see blue and red letters. When you

MONEY MAKING MATH | 63

press the shift keys, they will bring out the blue or the red buttons instead of the white ones.

For example, look at the top row. You will see the N button has a tiny red xP/YR under it. If you tap the red shift button, it makes the xP/YR bigger and allows you to use this instead of N. Same goes for the blue.

This calculator handles typing in all the formulas for you, all you have to do is populate the correct variables.

Don't get me wrong - I used to get chills when I thought of trying to use this calculator... but once someone explains how to use it, you figure out that it's not that difficult after all.

By the end of this chapter, you'll feel like Einstein because you're going to know everything you need to know about calculating the value of a note with this calculator.

Thankfully, you pretty much only need the top row.

N = Number of payments over the term of the loan. For instance, if you had a 30 year loan with 12 payments per year, it would be 360.

I/YR = interest rate/year. This is the rate of growth for your money. It can be interest rate, inflation, or yield. When you set this variable, make sure you use decimal numbers and not percentages. A 9% yield will be 9, not .09.

PV = Present Value of money. We mostly use this as the starting point for a loan. If you loan someone out 1000 bucks, then 1000 goes here.

PMT = The amount paid for each payment.

P/YR = Sets the number of payments made each year. Note, this is redshift PMT and you will always have it set to 12.

FV = future value of the money - what will be left on the loan. It is often 0 dollars when you are calculating from the start to the end, but there are cases when it won't be, such as for balloon loans.

A note on positive and negative: This calculator works by calculating the inflow and outflow of money. Outflow is negative on this calculator, meaning if it's negative then it is going out.

The reason I'm telling you this is because sometimes, you'll get a negative number. There's nothing wrong with the negative number, it just means the money is flowing out. Sometimes, you could get an error where the calculator complains about one of the numbers needing to be negative. This is fine too - it just means one of your variables needs to show money flowing out for the calculator to work properly.

For instance, if you're paying a PMT, that will have to be

negative in order to calculate the PV because the payment is going out of your bank account. Likewise, if your PV is what you are paying out, that will be negative in order to calculate the PMT. It doesn't really matter if PV or if PMT is negative, but one of them needs to be.

Don't worry if that was a little hard to understand - we're going to do plenty of examples.

CALCULATIONS

My grandparents retired to a life on a farm. If you've ever been to a farm, you know that farms need a lot of maintenance, one such maintenance item is cutting and hauling trees. I was in my mid-20's before my grandfather would let me use the chainsaw at his farm (He was a very cautious man).

I'll never forget the day he taught me. He was a spry 90 with all of the benefits of 2 knees surgeries and a hip replacement. I had never used a chainsaw before because I lived in the city and didn't really need to.

So, after he made me read the instruction manual, he decided that I was ready to give it a go. First, he started by demonstrating how to use it properly. Once he was satisfied that I knew what to do, he let me give it a try.

Since I'd never used one before, I didn't do a very great job. But I wasn't doing anything dangerous and I was getting the job done, so he sat back and quietly watched me learn how to use the tool.

After a few hours, I was a pro.

When we were finished, he told me the best way to show someone how to use a tool was to show them and shut up. Let them make their own mistakes and don't correct them unless they're doing something dangerous.

If you're wondering why I'm telling you this story, it's because that's exactly what we're going to do right now.

No, we're not cutting down trees - we're doing something even more exciting… calculating our yield!

The best way to learn something is to do it yourself, so I highly suggest you take out your calculator and some paper to work through these examples with me. If you haven't downloaded or purchased your 10bII calculator yet, shame on you! Do it now or you won't really learn. Trust me.

Let's say there's a $10,000 mortgage for 5 years at 10% interest. How much is the payment going to be?

On a sheet of paper, draw out a table that looks like the one below. N is the number of payments which is 5 years x 12 months. I/Yr is the interest rate and PV is the present value of 10,000. PMT is how much you will get per month. Easy enough, right?

Table 1

N	I/YR	PV	PMT
5 * 12	10	10,000	?

Now that you've drawn the table, enter these numbers into your calculator. To enter them in, type in the number then press the associated variable.

So, press 5 * 12 =. You should get 60. Now press the N at the top of the calculator. You should see 60 appear above the N. That means you've successfully loaded 60 into the N variable. If you go back to my picture, you'll see that 12 is above my N. That means that 12 is loaded in there.

Now, press 10 and then I/YR. Similarly, a 10 should appear above the I/YR button

Press 10000 and then press PV.

Since we want to calculate the PMT, we do not enter anything into the calculator for this variable. Just press the PMT button to see what the payment will be. You should get -212.47.

A negative!?

Remember our discussion about the inflow and outflow of money? It's negative because the payments are flowing out. That means we just did this calculation from the perspective of the borrower because they are the one paying 212.47 each month.

Unlike grade school, getting a negative answer when you expected a positive number doesn't really matter. It's the number that counts, not the signage.

If the negative bothers you, just make sure that you put the negative number in the appropriate variable.

If your number was a little off, it could be due to a few things.

1. These calculators do have rounding errors. Sometimes you'll be a few cents off. This is perfectly fine.
2. Your calculator may not be set to pay the payment at the end of the month.
3. Your P/YR might not be set to 12.

If you need to change your calculator to End Mode, press the red shift, then press the Beg/End button. In the top right, you will see "End" or "Beg" depending on what your calculator was on before. If you see "Beg" now, just do the sequence again.

MONEY MAKING MATH | 69

This button controls when the payment is paid. It can be paid at either the beginning or the end of the payment cycle. For mortgages, usually it's paid at the end of the cycle. This will not be cleared when you clear your calculator, so you likely never need to do it again.

If you need to change your P/YR to 12 type in 12, press red shift, then press P/YR. This also will not be cleared.

If you want to try that problem again, you'll need to clear your calculator. You can do this by pressing the red shift button and then pressing C. You need to do this each time you want to calculate something new.

Let's see if you got the hang of it. Now there's a $100,000 mortgage for 10 years at 18% interest. What will the payment be?

Try to draw your table before you look at mine!

Table 2

N	I/YR	PV	PMT
10 * 12	18	100,000	?

Did you get the above? Good! What was your answer? Mine was -1801.85.

These problems are pretty fun, but you might be wondering what the big deal is? All we've done is find payments.

The good news is you don't need to stick to finding the payment amount, you can find any of the variables. That means we can start to calculate something that is actually exciting- like the yield!

Let's say you come across Jim, a note holder that wants to send his son to college. Jim decided that he was going to sell one of his notes to help pay for it. He wants the money now, so he's willing to give you a pretty good deal. He tells you the borrower is paying 1801.95 every month for a term of 10 years. He wants to sell you this note for $75,000. What is your yield?

Table 3

N	I/YR	PV	PMT
10 * 12	?	-75,000	1801.95

You should get a 26.79% yield. You're buying this note for a great price!

What if the borrower already paid a few payments and you want to determine what the remaining balance is? It's pretty simple - you subtract the number of payments made from N and then solve for PV.

The borrower has been paying for 10 years. They originally had a loan for $300,000 at a 4% interest rate. They chose to go with a 30 year loan. How much is left on the note?

This problem is actually 2 steps. Try it for yourself before you look at my chart below.

Table 4

N	I/YR	PV	PMT
30 * 12	4	300,000	?
360	4	300,000	-1432.25
360-(12*10)	4	?	-1432.25
240	4	236,351.88	-1432.25

Neat, right? I found out what their payment is (because I didn't know that originally) and then I subtracted the 10 years of payments they'd already made from how many payments they had left. (12 months for 10 years is 120. 360-120 is 240). All I had to do after that was push the PV button to see what they have left on their mortgage.

This is also the formula for figuring out Balloon payments. All you would have to do is put the time in which the balloon pops in N. You would subtract that from the total loan time like we did with the (12*10) figure.

Let's do an example. You have a balloon loan that pops in 10 years. Your loan is $300,000 for 30 years at 4%. What are you going to owe when the balloon pops?

Table 5

N	I/YR	PV	PMT
30 * 12	4	300,000	?
360	4	300,000	-1432.25
360-(12*10)	4	?	-1432.25
240	4	236,351.88	-1432.25

As you can see, we did the exact same calculation. And in 10 years, you're going to owe $236,351. Better refinance!

How exciting! You learned how to use a new tool and now you can do simple calculations. I hope you're feeling a little more confident because these calculations are what you will use to perform due diligence.

One of the steps of due diligence is to calculate the yield of a few different exit strategies. Let's do an example where we calculate yield below.

Let's say you have a note that is for $100,000 for a 10 year term. The borrower pays 1060.66 each payment. What kind of rate of return would you like to make on this loan? Let's see what we would pay for this loan if we wanted to make 10%, 20%, and 30% yield.

Table 6

N	I/YR	PV	PMT
10 * 12	10	?	-1060.66
120	10	80,261.01	-1060.66
120	20	?	-1060.66
120	20	54,883.52	-1060.66
120	30	?	-1060.66
120	30	40,234.56	-1060.66

When you purchase a mortgage, you can use this same calculation to determine what you will make when you pay for it. If someone is offering a mortgage that pays 1060.66 per month for the next 10 years at 54,883, you know you'll get a 20% yield if you purchase that mortgage. Similarly, you can use this calculation when selling your note - especially when you are selling *partials*.

Selling partials is exactly what it sounds like - you don't sell the whole note... you just sell part of it. I know you probably have a few questions like *Who would actually buy that?* And *Why in the world would I do that?*

It's actually a pretty common technique amongst note investors. For instance, if you're starting with $0 but you find a really great note, you can sell part of it to another investor in order to pay for it.

This is another example of investing in the spread. You'd put no money down in exchange for less of a profit. As for others, well as we say in the note business, there are no bad notes, only bad deals. People don't care about only owning a partial, they just care about their yield.

Let's do an example together in case you come across this situation.

Say you've found a second position note for $6000. The payment every month is $158.17. You negotiated this note down to a great price and are going to make a 30% yield... that is, you would make a 30% yield if you had the money to buy it! Dangit!

What can you do?

The answer is obvious - you start looking for people who have $6000 and will accept a lower yield than 30%.

You easily find an investor in one of your REIAs who will accept a 23% yield for a $6000 investment. Now you need to find out how many payments will give him a 23% yield.

Table 7

N	I/YR	PV	PMT
?	23	6000	-158.17
68	23	6000	-158.17

It's only going to take a little over half the term of the loan to pay off his investment! That means you're still going to have 53 payments left. In about 5 years, you'll have turned your 0 dollar investment into an infinite return. And the person you sold the first half to is also getting an amazing deal. Who wouldn't want a 23% yield?

What if you wanted to sell the second half of the payments too because you figure if the first half is worth that much then the second half is probably also worth about that much. Besides, who wants to wait 5 years anyway.

The future value is going to come in handy for calculations like this where we need to know what a future amount will be worth.

First, we have to figure out what the loan will be at the end of this term. The terms of the second position lien are $14,912 for 5% interest amortized over a 10 year period. The payments are still $158.17/month. First, let's figure out how much will be left on the loan after 68 months.

Table 8

N	I/YR	PV	PMT	FV
68	5	?	158.17	-
68	5	9,349.28	158.17	-

76 | INVEST LIKE A BANK

We used the interest rate that the borrower is paying because we wanted to figure out what they had left on their loan. We know at the end of this period that we will have paid the other investor 6000 at a 23% yield. But all this time, our borrower was working on a $14,912 loan at 5% interest.

Now that we know what this loan is worth, we can calculate the second half of the payments!

Table 9

N	I/YR	PV	PMT	FV
68	23	?	-158.17	9349.28
68	23	3411.98	-158.17	9349.28

Do you see what I did there? I put the present value we calculated earlier into the future value spot because that's what the loan is going to be worth when there are only 68 payments left. Once I did that, I put the yield that we want our second half investor to make. We want them to have as great of a deal as our first investor because we want them to keep investing with us. Once the 23% was in there, I calculated the present value.

Holy cow! That's so low! Why would it be so low? That is the problem with the time value of money. The further out things are, the less it's worth because of inflation and amortized interest. But, when you think about it - you realize you invested a grand total of $0 into this loan and you got almost $3500 out of it! Not bad. Now you can take that $3500 and invest in some notes that you can keep!

Another concept I'd like to cover before we close this chapter is calculating what a balloon is worth. There are 2 parts to the balloon, the first part where you are receiving payments and the second part where the balloon pops and you are paid a lump sum. If you were to purchase a balloon loan, you would need to calculate both of these.

Let's say you found a loan for $200,000 that is amortized over 30 years with a balloon at the end of 15. The interest rate is 4%. We're experienced note investors so we know that we need to be patient and wait for the best deals. We won't accept this mortgage for anything less than a 20% yield. What should we pay for it?

Table 10

N	I/YR	PV	PMT	FV
12*30	4	200,000	?	-
360	4	200,000	-954.83	-

The first step should be familiar. We just need to find the

payment they make every month. For that, we use their interest rate and their timeline. The next step is finding out how much is left on the balloon when it pops.

Table 11

N	I/YR	PV	PMT	FV
12*15	4	?	-954.83	-
180	4	129,085.60	-954.83	-

So, when the balloon pops, it's worth 129,085.60. Now that we know everything about both parts of the loan, we can figure out what it will be worth to us if we want to get a 20% yield. First, we want to figure out what the first half of the loan is. We know that it will only be a term of 15 years and we know that the borrower is paying $954/month. What's it worth?

Table 12

N	I/YR	PV	PMT	FV
12*15	20	?	-954.83	-
180	20	54,366.14	-954.83	-

Great! We know that we would be willing to pay 54,366.14 for that first portion of it. Keep that number somewhere because we're going to need it later. Now, we want to figure out what we are going to pay for the popped part of the balloon.

Remember, 0$/month will be coming in when you get the popped portion. It's not going to be amortized over a period of time, it's just coming in all at once.

Table 13

N	I/YR	PV	PMT	FV
12*15	20	?	0	129,085.60
180	20	6,587.65	0	129,085.60

I don't know about you, but that number seems low! That's the price you pay for the time value of money. In 15 years, if we wanted to get a 20% return, the entire balance of that loan is only worth a fraction of the cost. First off, because we will not be getting any interest from it. Secondly because of inflation.

So, overall, we'd purchase this balloon loan for 54,366 + 6,587 = 60,953. Of course, if you wanted to get less of a return for that popped balloon, then the number would obviously be higher. If you're curious, you can do the same calculation for a 5% return, a 10% return, and a 15% return.

Pretty neat right?

80 | INVEST LIKE A BANK

The final concept I will show you here is for a step mortgage. A step mortgage is when the mortgage slowly raises every x number of years. So, let's say the mortgage originated to someone who thinks they will be able to pay more as time goes on because their job gives them a 3% raise each year.

Suppose you find a 3 year note that has a $100 step increase every year. The first year, they are paying $200/month. The second, they would pay $300/month and the third, they would pay $400/month.

First, we need to figure out what they are going to pay for the first year. This is the same thing we've been doing for the past hour, so you should be pretty good at it by now. We want to calculate what this mortgage is worth to us, so we are going to use our standard 20% rate.

Table 14

N	I/YR	PV	PMT	FV
12	20	?	200	-
12	20	-2159.02	200	-

Looks like that first year is going to be worth 2159. Now, we will calculate the second year. Remember, it's in the future so we have to use a future value.

Table 15

N	I/YR	PV	PMT	FV
12	20	?	300	-
12	20	-3238.53	300	-
12	20	?	0	3238.53
12	20	-2655.86	0	3238.53

Line 1 and 2 are used to find the future value. Use N to say how many payments this particular part of the note will pay out for the yield you want. This one will pay out 1 year for 12 payments. Once you've found that, you have the future value. Now, you would treat it as a balloon payment and use the time that has passed in order to find out what this future value of 3238.53 is worth.

You will have to wait 12 months (1 year) for this part of the loan to start paying, so you put 12 in the N column on line 3. We still want a 20% yield, so we keep that in I/YR. We move the PV from line 2 to the PV in line 3 and solve for the new present value. What's that future payment worth now?

Now, we will do the third year. I think this year will really help you understand what is going on here.

Table 16

N	I/YR	PV	PMT	FV
12	20	?	400	-
12	20	-4318.05	400	-
24	20	?	0	4318.05
24	20	-2904.03	0	4318.05

Cool! Now we can add up all of these present values and get the value of this loan. 2159.02 + 2655.86 + 2904.03 = 7718.91

4

THE 7 BEST PLACES TO FIND NOTES

This business is all about finding notes. It doesn't matter how much money you have, if you find a good investment, you can find an interested investor. As you send this investor more great deals, you build trust and that trust turns into a relationship. That is why actually finding the notes is the most important thing you can do for your business - it's your bread and butter.

In this chapter, I will share 7 strategies you can use to find notes. Each strategy lends itself to finding a different type of note - so you'll probably be limited to 1 or 2 of them based on what kind of note you decided to invest in in chapter 2.

ONLINE NOTES EXCHANGES

Online marketplaces are like a catch-22. You can find notes on there for very little work, but you don't make as much profit and you need a lot of money to get started. If you're scared to start calling people and you have the money, this is a great place to get your feet wet. Keep in mind, these marketplaces are better for the seller than they are the buyer because the notes have usually been marked up - which means this is not a great place to start if you want to broker notes

Another downside to using these note exchanges is that they are often short lived. For whatever reason, they tend to go offline after a few years which will leave you searching for another market. At the time of this writing, all of the websites I mention are up and doing deals. That might not be the case in the future when you go through this - so I am going to list a few of them.

NotesDirect.com

Notes direct sells both performing and non-performing notes in residential and commercial locations. When you join, you join their email list where they email out interesting notes every month.

They offer a lot of information about the note which makes

performing cursory due diligence very easy. However, you should get into the habit of verifying information if you are seriously looking into purchasing a note. No matter who is trying to sell it to you.

When I first started learning about investing in notes, I heard some advice that really stuck with me: Treat all note investors like crooks. I know what it sounds like - it sounds like you're about to start investing in an asset that attracts criminals - but that's not the case at all!

Not all note investors are crooks, in fact most of them are very honest people… but you need to verify all of the information they give you. You are the arbiter of your own destiny and no one cares about your money like you do. So, you need to verify everything anyone tells you. Even if they don't mean to lie to you, they could still give you bad information.

The downsides of NotesDirect are that it isn't a streamlined process, the checklist of what you need to do isn't great, and you have to hire your own servicing company.

But, if you want to start investing, this is a great place to get your feet wet. It takes away the hardest part of note investing - finding notes.

So, how does NotesDirect work?

First, you go to their website and sign up. Once you've filled out their initial application, you go through the approval process. If you are approved, you enter in more information and go through a tertiary approval process.

Once you are in, you will be able to see all of the performing notes they have listed. To see non-performing notes, you will need to gain some experience because they don't allow brand new note investors to take on the "risk" of non-performing notes right off the bat. A sentiment I can agree with.

Once you've found a note that you like and performed due diligence, they give you a checklist to work through. This is great for new investors because it gives you the confidence to know that you're doing the right steps in the right order.

The price is fixed so there's no negotiation or bidding and you need to pay all the money upfront. All of this lends itself towards actually investing in a note as opposed to brokering it, so if your strategy was to broker a few, you might want to pass on this opportunity for now. Once you buy a note, you have to pay closing costs and the $750 processing fee from NotesDirect.

If you have the money and want to invest in a few performing notes, this is a great place to start. You can make some pretty good returns from just investing in these performing notes. And, if you start with an easy investment, it gets your confidence up and lets you go through the paperwork process in a relatively safe environment. Like I said in chapter 2, this is a great way for new investors to get started because it will guide you through the process and give you confidence in a relatively safe, controlled environment.

WatermarkExchange.com

Watermark Exchange is another aggregation website. Admittedly, they have more non-performing notes than performing and are much more focused on residential than commercial.

The registration process for watermark is a lot less stringent than NotesDirect. Once you have signed up, they let you see all of their notes. You can either peruse all of their notes or you can filter them: performing or non-performing notes, the lien position, sale type, and state/city.

Once you've found a note of interest and have completed your due diligence, you can make an offer. All offers are emailed to the owner of the site and will take a few days to process.

PeerStreet.com/PatchOfLand.com/Blackhawkinvesting.com

I've lumped these sites together because they're very similar.

They are not like the other two because you have to be an accredited investor. An accredited investor is someone who either earns more than $200,000 per year ($300,000 if you're a married couple) or has a net worth over $1 million. If this sounds like you and you like super passive investing, then this might be your choice.

These websites boast of an ROI of 5%-11%. It's not the fastest way to get rich but it is a "secure" investment. If you just want to park some funds into notes, then these websites are perfect for you.

BANKS/CREDIT UNIONS

The thought of talking to banks can be a little daunting when you first start out. However, if you stick to it, you will find that it is the most profitable way to invest in notes. The main goal of speaking with banks is to set up a pipeline of non-performing note tapes for pennies on the dollar.

Think about it - banks originate loans every day. People default on their loans every day - believe me, one look at your county's foreclosure list for the month is enough to make your heart sink. Luckily, if you get a bank's tape, you can help these distressed borrowers better than a bank ever could.

Banks often do not try to negotiate a new loan with a delinquent borrower unless it is ordered by the court. When their borrower misses enough payments to make their investment unprofitable, they simply foreclose.

Banks are inherently heartless.

They only look at their bottom line and are heavily regulated. If they are unprofitable or do something that seems untoward, there is a high chance that they will be audited.

Believe me when I say that banks fear nothing as much as they fear being audited. It's a major drain on their resources and can literally shut them down.

So, banks usually foreclose if one of their borrowers becomes delinquent. They don't have time to play with their borrowers. Foreclosure is a long, drawn out process and often means more fees (legal, realtor, auction), a long waiting period, and has a surprising high risk of vandalism. Foreclosing is not a fun process for anyone and it's extremely unprofitable. So, it's better for banks to sell their non-performing notes. They'll make back some of their money and it will be far faster.

If you want to call banks, your focus should be on local banks. By local, I mean small banks. They don't necessarily have to be local to you, but they have to be local to the area as opposed to a huge franchise. You should never call one of the top 20 banks - they're just too big. If you try, you'll probably never find anyone that can help because all the people you need to talk to are too busy.

Local banks are completely different. Less people work in management and there is less going on at any time so you will be able to find someone who can help you relatively quickly. This is great news because there are over 10,000 small banks and credit unions in the US.

The better news (for you, anyway) is that they have less money to leverage so they invest in less notes.

That might sound like bad news because they will have less notes on their tapes, but that also means that a single npn can harm their bottom line more than it ever would at a large bank. I.e. they care more than big banks about selling their npns as quickly as possible to avoid becoming unprofitable or being audited. So, they're more willing to sell you their npns! You'd be doing them a huge favor.

That's why we're going to call the small, local or regional banks around the country.

So, now that we have an idea of which banks we're going to call, who in the bank will we try to speak with?

The executives!

That's right! We're going to start with the presidents and vice presidents of the bank.

Why? Because they will understand what you're trying to help you with.

The President of the bank is well aware of how notes work and, though he might not be the right person, he can transfer you to the executive you need to speak with.

Try walking into a bank and asking a clerk about their portfolio of npns. They won't know what that is and will likely tell you that their bank doesn't do that.

Very few people know about notes - that's why this investment model is so lucrative!

So now that you know you need to talk to people who know about these notes, you might be wondering why you have to call the president (or vice president) of these banks. Why not just call the person responsible for the notes? The answer to that is two-fold.

First, the positions and processes are not standardized. Each bank is kind of just doing their own thing. That means that no one can tell you who exactly is responsible for the notes for each individual bank except for the people that work there.

Secondly, if you get someone's boss to transfer you to them, they'll actually take you seriously.

If I was to call your boss right now and say "I need to talk to someone responsible for…" and he told you to talk to me, don't you think you'd care a little more than if some random person off the street started asking you a question?

So, now that we know we need to talk to executives, we need to talk about how to talk to them. Most people feel nervous about talking to bank execs. After all, aren't they the bad guy in all our Saturday morning cartoons? Aren't they the evil soul sucking leeches that charge us late fees and don't listen to reason? Don't they pinch their luxurious mustaches as they dive into their pool of gold coins?

Well… yeah I guess. But don't you want a pool of gold coins?

Kidding. Kidding.

But seriously, remember that you are starting your own business. Just think of it this way - those banks need help recovering some of their investment. You are there to help them offload a few bad investments so they can stay afloat for another year. In the process, you have the potential to help all of those people that might have slipped through the cracks.

Don't worry about the title of whoever it is you're calling. If you ran into them in a park, would you care that they were the President of Wisconsin First Bank? They put their pants on one leg at a time and they need your help.

Besides, 9 times out of 10 you'll be talking with their secretary anyway.

Once you find a bank that wants to work with you, make sure you do everything you can to maintain a good relationship. Answer their calls after hours, respond to their emails promptly, and do not try to haggle down their price.

Why?

Because you want this bank to be a repeat customer! They aren't just going to have one bad month of non-performing notes... they're going to have non-performing notes for as long as they are a bank! And you want them to think of you when they need to offload them.

Once you establish a good, working relationship, you just have to remind them that you still exist every now and then and they will send you another tape of non-performing notes you can sell.

BOOM!

All of a sudden, you don't have to do as much work to find notes. If you have 4 or 5 banks, you could be set for a long time with an advertising budget of near $0.

Of course, this takes a lot of work to set up. First, you have to find the banks. Then you have to find someone who will talk to you (I didn't say it would be easy, I just said it would be possible!). Then you have to find *the right* person to talk to.

You'll probably have to call their office 10 times before they even get back to you. I'm sorry to say it, but that's just how busy people are. Busy people are busy. Of course, even when you find the right person and get a return call, they may not have any non-performing notes at the time. That's ok, all you have to do is wait and send them a postcard or give them a call every now and then. I'll tell you more about that at the end of this chapter in the section titled "A Note on Relationship Building".

It's a lot of work! It will take you several weeks of cold calling to find one customer… but you will find them. And the more you cold call, the better you get!

Your first step is to get a list of banks in the United States. You can do that here: https://www.bankbranchlocator.com/banks-in-usa.html. Similarly, here are all the credit unions: https://www.creditunionsonline.com/search_usa.html. Pick 100 out.

Got 100 picked out? Good! All you have to do now is start searching for the executive's phone numbers, email addresses, and linked-ins. You don't need to call all 100 of them today (good lord no!) just call 10. Just make it a goal to give 10 a call each day.

Do this for a few weeks. Some of the banks will tell you that they don't have any notes now, but that you need to call them later. Make sure you follow up with them at that later date!

Sometimes, you'll talk with an executive who is not the right person, but knows who is. They'll transfer you over or give you a name and number.

This is exactly what you want!

You want to get a hold of the person who handles all of the *non-accruals loans*. When that happens, call them right away and let them know that <Name>, the <Title>, told you to talk to them. That's why we start high in the chain. It's easier to work your way down than work your way up.

Calling and speaking with bank execs is a very deep topic in this niche. There are certain words they use that investors don't necessarily use. Here are the basics.

Each bank has a pool of performing and non-performing notes. This pool is called a *portfolio*. If you have a mortgage, you are in that bank's portfolio. Within this portfolio are smaller portfolios of notes called *buckets*.

The 3 buckets that we care about are the 30 to 89 day late bucket, the 90+ day late bucket, and the Nonaccrual bucket. These are loans that haven't been paid for some time and are either at risk of not accruing or are currently not accruing any money.

The loans that are 30 - 90 days late are still considered accruing because the bank hasn't given up on the borrower yet. In fact, the bank is still charging the borrower interest and late fees. Once the borrower has 90 days of delinquent payments, banks start to classify them as non-accrual. It's considered a loss in their books which causes the process for foreclosure to begin.

Why would a bank do this? Because it is statistically unlikely for that borrower to ever catch up after that. Not without some kind of payment plan which normally only occurs when the borrower is being faced with foreclosure.

So, when you call a bank, you should ask if you can help them get any of their non-accruing loans off their books. Do not ask for non-performing notes. They likely don't know what you're talking about.

If you do choose to go this route, expect to be on the phone for a few weeks or months before you find something viable. You'll probably need to make some kind of contact with 1 executive 8 times before they answer you.

Like all cold calling, you need to be persistent! And, for the love of all that is good, be nice to their secretary. She will be the one you are speaking with most often and a happy secretary is more likely to pass your message along.

LEVERAGING LINKEDIN

There are entire books and courses out there that teach you how to use LinkedIn. It's one of the newest ways to find and build your investor network! LinkedIn is all about making connections and expanding your network. You will be using it specifically to link up with people who want to buy or sell (or both) notes from you.

The method I am going to share with you will work for both connecting with investors and connecting with financial professionals. I will show you how to use LinkedIn so that people think about you when it's time for their bank, credit union, or hedge fund to dump some notes.

The method in question leverages your current relationships to create new ones. Research proves that the best way to make a new business or personal connection is a warm introduction. And that's exactly what we're going to get.

Using a warm introduction on LinkedIn is known to have a success rate of over 60%. So theoretically, for every 10 people you message, 6 of them will want to connect with you. That's much better than calling 8 times to get in touch with one person! The downside is that you have to have a

LinkedIn account set up and need a few connections to get started.

If you don't have a LinkedIn account set up, the best advice I can give you is to start going to REI clubs in your local area, collecting business cards, and connecting with people on LinkedIn. You should be able to get 20 or 30 connections from your meetups alone. Start connecting with everyone you know in real life as well - it doesn't matter who they are or how long it's been since you've spoken last, they could know someone you want to get in touch with.

If you follow this advice, you should net quite a few connections. Again, it doesn't matter what their profession is, all that matters is you have them as a connection. Random people know random people. And some of those random people are people you want to connect with!

Now that we have that out of the way, let's move on to the actual strategy.

One cool thing about LinkedIn is it keeps track of how many connections you are away from someone else. A second degree connection with Bob means you don't know Bob but you know at least one person who does. A third degree would be if Bob knows Cindy. You don't know Bob or Cindy but you know someone who knows Bob.

Once you have signed up for your free LinkedIn account,

you need to set it up. Make sure your profile appears professional. You should have a professional headshot or business logo as your profile picture and a 100% complete profile. Don't worry, LinkedIn will walk you through the steps for this.

Remember, we are connecting with real people and they want to get a feel for who you are before they do business with you. Some of them will look at your profile to determine if you are worth their time. Make sure you come off as put together, knowledgeable, and reliable.

Now that everything is set up, the fun begins! The LinkedIn strategy is simple: look for a second degree connection that can help you and then ask for a warm introduction from your first degree connection.

Before I start walking you through how to do this, I want to remind you that LinkedIn is a huge tech company. As such, their website and rules are always changing. I will do my best to keep up but something is bound to get out of date. Please bear with me if this is the case!

Step 1. Find a second degree connection

There's a search bar on the top left of the page next to their logo. When you click in there, a drop down appears. Along the top of the dropdown, you should see the word "People". Click on that.

LinkedIn should load a new page that shows you some people. You probably know some of them. There should be a white bar across the top. On the right of that white bar, you'll see the words "All Filters". Click on that.

Select "2nd" under connections. Select the United States as the country. Leave the sections talking about companies alone. Under Industries, type in the following words one by one and check all of the search terms that appear in the drop down.

> *Bank*
> *Investment*
> *Capital Markets*
> *Commercial*
> *Financial*

After checking all of the keywords that appeared from the above, I have Financial Services, Commercial Real Estate, Capital Markets, Investment Management, Investment Banking, Banking...

This is not an exhaustive list but it's enough to get you started. You can also target real estate agents, title companies, lawyers, accountants and bank trust officers. All of these groups come across notes frequently.

Scroll down until you see a bunch of white text boxes. You

should see one that says Title. Type in "president" or "CEO" or "Executive".

If you'd like, you can type "Asset Manager" in the top search bar. It should bring up some people who actually manage assets for their companies. But if you don't see enough of them, then it's fine to leave it as it was before.

Step 2. Reach out to your first degree connections

Here's the heart of this method: LinkedIn will tell you who the first degree connection is for each of these second degree connections. Now, you need to reach out to your first degree connection and ask them if you can mention their name in an introduction to the second degree connection. Your message should be something like the following:

Bob,

I noticed you're connected to Tara Smith and I'd like to reach out to her. Do you mind if I mention your name?

Hope business is booming!

Thanks,

Beaux

Bob is the first degree connection you have (The person you know). Tara Smith is the second degree connection you have (The person you want to connect with) and your name should go where mine is.

Don't change the above message too much. It's short, sweet, and gets the point across. You only need to explain what you are doing if they ask why. You don't want to overload them with a huge message because remember, busy people are busy. They probably don't want to read more than a few sentences.

If Bob gives you the go-ahead, great! We will be using our relationship with him to introduce ourselves to Tara.

It's very tempting to immediately send Tara a connection request with a message telling her why you're contacting her.

Do not do this.

Why?

Because we are going to repeat this thousands of times a month. Remember, this method only has a 60% success rate. That means 40% will either ignore you or decline your message.

After a certain number of them have declined, Linkedin will start to throttle your account which means you won't be able to send connection requests anymore. This obviously limits your ability to make connections in the future and will throttle your business.

That brings us to step 3!

Step 3. Connect with the Second Degree Connection

Sadly, even if you pony up for a premium account, LinkedIn will only let you message a few people each day.

Fortunately for us, there is a way around LinkedIn's rules - if you share a group with another person, you can DM them. So, the next step is to find what groups your second degree connection belongs to. From now on, I'm going to call my second-degree connection Tara because I think it makes it easier to follow.

Luckily, you don't need to be connected with someone to look at their LinkedIn profile, which is how we will find out which groups Tara belongs to. Click on Tara's name. It's going to bring you to her profile.

Scroll all the way to the bottom to her interests section. Select See All. there should be a pop-up where you can see groups. Click on "Groups". If they have any groups, find an open group and join it.

After the open group has accepted you, you can search the members for Tara.

To do that, go to that group's page. In the top right, you'll see a tile with members in it. Click on "See All". Now, a bunch of people who belong to this group should pop up. Search for Tara and then click on "Message" on the right.

Here is my template for talking to Bank Executives. You might need to tweak it a bit for other groups, but it's a great starting point.

Hi Tara,

I saw that we're both connected to Bob and wanted to reach out. I told him I'd be reaching out to you, and he thought it would be a good connection.

It would be great to chat sometime about how I could help your bank liquidate your non-accrual loans.

Thanks,

Beaux

Make sure you send the same message to each type of

connection. For instance, send the same message to everyone who is a bank executive. Craft a different message and send that one to everyone who is a real estate agent. You might need to change a few words like "Bank" to "Credit Union" but in the end, your general message should be the same.

If you start getting a bunch of declines, then you know your message isn't good enough. If people start biting, then you know you have a great message. Like most things, it's all about advertising!

When someone directs you to their asset manager, or whatever their credit union/bank/company calls them, you need to enter their information into your CRM and contact them on a regular cadence.

Your CRM could be an excel spreadsheet with the name, date of contact, contact number, address, and day to call again. It could also be fancier software that also sends you a message to remind you to call them on a certain date automatically. The choice is yours.

Remember, getting a tape is about knowing the right people and talking to them at the right time. They might not have anything when you first connect, but don't give up! That could change in a few months.

Calling frequently is one method of making these note

professionals call you when they need to sell a note. And you should definitely include this in your strategy because when you contact them regularly, they will think of you because you'll be fresh on their mind. But, there is another way that you can remind them you exist - Posting. A lot.

If people are on LinkedIn a lot, they will see your posts. You should post on both your feed and in groups.

When you post, don't just spam the groups with "I'm gonna buy your notes!" messages. Make sure you also post useful information. Read about what is happening in the banking world and in the note world and make sure you post helpful articles. It will make you look knowledgeable and professional as well as remind your target audience that you buy notes.

You may be able to find someone on Fiverr.com to take care of your social media posts for you. If you do, make sure you look for a level 2 seller who actually has some knowledge on notes. Alternatively, you can schedule some posts on your feed or just sit down every saturday and post all of the articles to the groups.

Make sure the groups you join to post in have your customer base, not your competitors. If you can join banking LinkedIn groups, financial LinkedIn groups, etc then you'll have a better shot at the right people seeing your posts.

Sure, the note groups are great for talking with other note investors and staying up to date on note information... but they are not your intended audience. They are your competition, so posting in their groups doesn't do you much good when it comes to finding notes.

ATTENDING CONFERENCES

Like I said, this business is all about relationships. Not only will conferences (many of which cost less than $1000 to attend) help you learn more about this business, they will also help you connect with more note brokers and other people in the field. As we saw from our LinkedIn exercise earlier, the more connections you have, the more connections you can make.

Some of the more popular conferences can be found at:

- NoteExpo.com
- Papersourceseminars.com
- Noteworthysummit.com

Try to attend one conference in your first year. It's more than enough to get you going. If you're worried about how much it will cost you, keep in mind that you can expense it and get some of that money back as a tax return.

SELLER-FINANCED NOTES

Seller financed notes are loans that were originated from an individual instead of a bank. For example, when a house is sold, the buyer usually does not have all of the funds necessary to buy it, so they must find a bank to originate a mortgage.

If the buyer has bad credit or does not have money for a down payment, they need to find some other way to pay. Unless you've been investing for a while, you've probably never heard of seller financing before. You'll be surprised to learn that it's actually pretty popular, all things considered.

Over half a million mortgages are originated each month and about 5% of all real estate deals are seller financed each year. 5% of 500,000 is 25,000 seller financed mortgages *per month*. So there is definitely a market.

Originating Notes

Now that we know we can purchase these seller financed notes from random people, how do we find them? Same as every other strategy - we set up a pipeline.

First, we need to figure out who knows about our Seller Financed notes - realtors, title companies, attorneys, and servicing companies.

Each of these professions come across notes frequently and sometimes the notes are even for sale. Now that you have your targeted audience, you need to start advertising yourself as "The Note Guy". The best way you can do this is by being useful to their business.

For instance, if a realtor is dealing with a buyer who wants to buy a house but can't get financed - you can offer the solution to them. That would be very useful to the realtor because they don't make any money unless they actually sell a house. And if someone has bad credit, they probably don't have all the money they need to purchase one.

A quick note on originating notes before we continue: this book does not talk about originating loans at all. However, most states allow an individual to originate 1 loan per year without a license or a business entity. If you want to go this route, you will need to do a little more research on your own or speak to an attorney. It's doable - it's just too in depth to put in this book.

Back to actually finding these seller financed notes. You can start by calling (or connecting via LinkedIn) realtors, title companies, attorneys, and servicing companies in the areas you're trying to invest. When you connect with them, ask if they have seen any hard to close notes recently. Tell them that you can close almost any note.

Buying Originated Notes

If you want to find notes that are already seller financed - which I recommend if you're first starting out - go on CraigsList or FaceBook Marketplace and search for "Seller Finance". The listings that pop up will be investors who will finance out their investments. You can give them a call and let them know you buy notes. Don't be pushy, but let them know that if they ever want to sell, you're their guy!

Like calling banks, you're going to have to call 100 of these realtors, companies and investors several times before you find one that is willing to work with you. That said, it will all be more than worth it when they immediately call you with a note they need help with or want to sell.

Embrace the discomfort and get good at making connections. Be persistent and useful! And when you can't be useful, just work on making a personal connection (More on that at the end of the chapter).

If you aren't having any luck with realtors, title companies or other investors, there is still hope! You can purchase a list of seller financed note holders for a pretty cheap price from listsource.com.

Listsource calls seller financed notes carrybacks, but it's pretty much the same thing. Make sure you have an idea of which are you want to invest in before you try to buy a list from ListSource, though. You pay by the lead.

When you get your list from listsource, there are 2 main things you can do: Set up a mailer campaign or skip trace and cold call.

Mailer

If you do a mailer campaign, I recommend you use click2-mail.com. You can set up a mail campaign here for an extremely reasonable price.

When you set up a mail campaign, you should start with a compelling letter and then send a postcard for the next 5 weeks. After that, send a postcard once a month. You want to include messaging that suggests you buy notes. Some great phrases are "Need to sell a property quickly, even in a slow market?" or "Searching for ways to maximize sale price and build future income?".

Even if they don't answer your mailer immediately, chances are some of them will keep it for when they need it.

Cold Calling

If you would rather call them, I recommend you use reiskip.com to skiptrace their phone numbers. Once you have their number, you should follow up at least once a month for a few months. If they ask that you stop calling them, stop calling them and remove them from your list.

You can, of course, combine the two strategies if you want. I'd suggest calling everyone on your list first and then sending a mailer to remind them of who you are. It doesn't really matter how you follow up as long as you do actually follow up.

FDIC LOAN SALES

Remember how I said banks were terrified of getting audited? Well, the FDIC loan sales are notes that were originated by banks that have been audited and penalized for failing the audit.

The FDIC is a government agency that protects your money from banks that make poor choices. Every bank account in every reputable bank is insured up to a certain amount through the FDIC. So, if the bank makes a string of bad investments, over leverages, or goes under for any reason they can't just take your money. The FDIC makes sure that you still have it.

After a bank fails, the FDIC takes over all of their assets. You can purchase these assets when the FDIC holds a sale. They range from single assets to huge tapes. This is a great place to go if you have money to invest because you can't legally broker the FDIC lists. Of course, you'll need to be approved before you can participate.

HEDGE FUNDS AND NOTE BROKERS

Becoming a hedge fund is the dream of every note investor. Everyone wants a business that moves millions of dollars worth of notes every year and pays their investors a share of it.

Hedge funds invest their investor's money in tapes of (usually) non-performing notes. They often have millions of dollars of other people's money (OPM) at their disposal. When they receive these npns, they foreclose, workout, or sell them based on how profitable they project them to be.

If you're investing in a hedge fund, you take part in all their profits. Unfortunately, you usually need to be an accredited investor to do this. However, sometimes hedge funds will let non-accredited investors purchase one off notes from them.

If you do this, just know you're buying the deals they didn't think would be profitable. That's not to say they aren't, but be careful and make sure you perform all your due diligence before you buy.

Even though hedge funds deal with thousands of notes each year, they are not very regulated. Since they aren't regulated, it makes it pretty hard to find any of their information online… for free. Of course, if you want to pay a few thousand dollars for a list, then it's easy to figure out all the information you need to start contacting the executives of the hedge fund.

I really don't recommend a new note investor do this. Any of the other methods I've mentioned are leaps and bounds better than taking a hedge fund's leftovers.

Also worth mentioning is a network of small note brokers. These smaller companies don't usually ask investors for money - they are in the business of selling them to investors. This is what you want to do with your first few notes - broker them to other investors.

There are large, well known Note Brokers and there are smaller, less proven note brokers. Unfortunately, it is very easy for a new investor to get suckered into a broker chain, so I really want to caution you on purchasing notes from the smaller brokers. Make sure you have a little bit of experience before you trust an unproven note broker. Remember, all note investors are crooks!

Some of the larger, more trusted note brokers are DebtX, First Financial, and Mission Capital.

A word of caution - do not try to broker notes that you are purchasing from note brokers. If you are going to buy a note from a broker, make sure YOU are the one putting up the money to buy it. Don't try to pawn it off on another note investor.

Why not?

Because most of the profits will be eaten away from the first time the note was brokered. And it's also just really frowned upon in the note world. It's how you become known as a joker broker and damage your reputation.

A NOTE ON RELATIONSHIP BUILDING

My dad has been in sales for a while. The best advice he gave me about selling is to treat the voice on the other line like they are a human. Because they are.

Back in the day, my dad would keep a rolodex of his contacts.

For our younger readers, a rolodex is basically a book of flashcards where you kept contact information.

He would make frequent social calls to his buyers. He would talk to them like they were his best friends. If they wanted to chat, then he would get them chatting, if they were busy, he would state his business and then politely let them get off the phone. If at any point they mentioned a pet's name, a birthday, or a serious illness in the family, he'd write that down in his rolodex (Or if it was a date, his calendar).

When the birthday rolled around, he'd send a birthday card. He'd ask about their kids and pets. If they had a sick relative the last time they talked, maybe he'd ask how they were doing. If they weren't doing well or they had died, he'd send flowers.

Anything that was meaningful to his customer was meaningful to him. He understands something that a lot of new salespeople do not - banks and businesses might be cold, but the humans who work there are not.

Investing in notes is a people business. You need to create relationships with the people you talk to if you want repeat business. Going the extra mile and sending them a card on their birthday, a check in call to see how they're doing when a natural disaster hits their area, or simply asking about their dog is going to set you apart from other people.

You want to set yourself apart from other note investors. They might just send a monthly mailer and be done with it... but not you. You want to make human connections. You want people to become your friend so they think of you when notes roll across their desk. Is it a little more work? Yes - but it's worth it.

5

ASSEMBLING YOUR TEAM - JACK OF ALL TRADES, MASTER OF NONE.

When you start investing, you should invest all over the United States. Expanding beyond your town opens up a literal world of possibilities. Lots of investors get nervous when you suggest this because it's been drilled into their head that they have to physically see their investment in order to determine it's a good one.

The good news is: you don't need to! Note investors don't normally go see their investment unless it is millions of dollars.

Note investors also don't do everything themselves. Most have a team of people to support them. I'm not going to say it's impossible but it would be pretty damn hard for a single person to be an attorney, a title company, a realtor, and a servicer all at once. If you wanted to wear all of those hats for every note, be my guest. Just know that it's going to be extremely time consuming and you're going to make a lot of mistakes.

If you want to be a note investor(not broker), you need to hire a team of people.

You should stop thinking of yourself as a worker and start thinking of yourself as the CEO. The CEO doesn't write all the code, do all the marketing, or deal with legal... and neither will you. Your job is to find deals.

Pretty simple, right?

If note investors had to do everything themselves, I'm sure even fewer people would be investing in notes. It's just not sustainable or profitable. Your time is much better spent analyzing deals than sending out foreclosure letters or analyzing titles.

In fact, if I was to dedicate a chapter to everything everyone on your team does, this book would be a million pages and take 3 years to read.

With that out of the way, here are the different teammates you're going to need to make your note investing business run smoothly.

DOCUMENT CUSTODIAN

The first member of your team is a document custodian. Document custodians store your original documents in a locked safe. They will store them from the moment you start negotiating a payment with the seller all the way to when you decide to sell the note.

The flow is such: You and the note seller decide you want to do business with each other. The seller sends the documents to the document custodian. You hire someone to ensure the documents are authentic and nothing strange is going on with the Note. Once that has been done, you release the funds to the seller.

Like any business, there are scammers. You need to make sure everything is legitimate before you send them money. Document custodians help save your money from illegitimate investors because only release your money if the documents are proven to be authentic and problem free.

NEVER wire other note investors money. They're all Crooks.

Protect yourself. Use a document custodian to ensure the note is legitimate.

ATTORNEY

Attorneys are a very important part of your team. You need at least one attorney per investment state because they are up to date with all of the state's laws. You can also use your attorney to check the title if you don't trust a title company to do it.

Your attorney is also responsible for filing for foreclosure. This includes making sure you are in compliance with all the local laws and taking care of any snags along the way. They will send letters to your borrower reminding them that foreclosure is imminent. Attorneys are often part of a carrot and stick plan to make your borrowers call you back if they are delinquent. Obviously, they are the stick, prodding the borrower to call your servicer to make a deal (The carrot).

Attorneys are also there when you need legal advice. For instance, if you've invested in a property with an HOA lien, a mechanics lien, and a medical lien, you probably want to ask your attorney which of those will fall off.

Liens are tricky business. Some liens will fall off. Some liens will stay attached (even after foreclosure). Some liens can be negotiated down. Talk to your attorney, they are there to help you sort through those things.

Their job is to look at your situation from a legal perspective and give you legal counsel on your best path forward. You can find a Real Estate Specific Lawyer for any state at Legal-League100.com.

LICENSE SERVICER

Servicers manage collections and interactions with your borrowers. They will send letters, send emails and make phone calls. They make sure you get your money and send out all of the paperwork to keep you compliant with laws and regulations like CFPB rules, Dodd-Frank rules, RESPA, and many more.

If you don't want to hire a servicer, you better love cold calling, mailing notices, and reading about laws.

If you're dealing with an npn, then your servicers also serve another purpose: negotiator.

Servicers are the "carrot" in the carrot and stick approach to npns. The license servicer will try to work with the borrower to find a resolution that is a win/win for everyone. The reason the lawyer is involved is some borrowers will refuse to call your servicer back. They need to be reminded that the clock is ticking. It's sad, but sometimes it's necessary.

You can find a list of special servicers here: distressedpro.com/special-servicers-list/.

REALTOR

You want to have a cordial relationship with everyone on your team, but realtors can really make or break your business. You need to find a realtor that specializes in the zipcodes you are investing in. The more they know about the area, the better they will do their job.

Realtors deal with property all day so their opinion on what a particular home is worth is much more meaningful than information you find online. They also have their ear to the ground and can give you the insider scoop.

With any real estate business, it's best to find investor friendly realtors, so your first stop is meetup.com. You should search for real estate clubs in your target investment area. When you find a few REAI groups, go on their forums and search for comments and posts about realtors. You want to find the good ones and avoid the bad ones.

If you can't find any, you can contact the originator of the group and ask who they recommend or simply post your own question. Lots of realtors really don't like working with investors for one reason or another. Using meetup is the easiest way to find good, investor friendly realtors.

That said, if you can't find any meetups in that area, the next best thing is to go on zillow and search for houses that have recently sold. Zillow has this neat feature where they suggest realtors that have sold in the area.

After you look on Zillow, you should have a pool of 5-10 local realtors. Call each of them. Try to find one that you think you can work with because you will probably be working with them for a long time.

You can use more than one realtor per area, but be sure you give the realtors you work with business when you can. Oftentimes, they help investors for free. Their only benefit is the referral you send them.

Remember - if you help them, they'll help you! If they feel like you are screwing them, they are not going to continue to work with you.

TITLE COMPANY

You need to find a title company in your investment's state. You do not want to try to close your own deals in the note space - there's just too much that can go wrong. You need a trained eye to look through the paperwork and make sure that your current deal does not have anything fishy going on.

Closing through a title company will add an extra grand to your purchase price, but it's well worth the piece of mind that it was done correctly. They also give you insurance on the mortgage that takes care of anything unexpected. You should find a title company through the meetup message boards, as I described above. If you can't, then you should use google.

Title companies do not usually have the same stigma against investors as realtors, so don't be afraid to find one on your own. Almost all of them will do.

CERTIFIED PROFESSIONAL ACCOUNTANT

A CPA will make sure that your books are balanced, you pay your taxes, and you aren't doing anything illegal. If you get a CPA that has knowledge of the real estate world, they can also give you advice on different laws that will minimize your taxes and maximize your profits.

If you really are hard pressed, you could use a service like quickbooks in lieu of a CPA. However, try shopping around to find one first. They aren't usually that expensive to retain and will make your life much easier.

PROPERTY MANAGER

A good property manager is hard to come by, but well worth the hassle. If you can get advice on good property managers from the local REI club, then that's great! If not, you'll have to use yelp.

You should ask them how their payment structure operates, how responsive their company is to you and your renters, and how they would handle a disaster situation - like a hot water heater exploding. You should also ask them how they screen renters and if they are willing to help you steer clear of problem areas around the city.

If you never plan on renting out a house, then you might get away without a property manager. Just make sure the notes you buy are for properties in a strong market. Ask your realtor for a market report to find out.

BOOTS ON THE GROUND

Last, but not least, you need someone to go take pictures of the house. You need to make sure your investment is still there and that it is in good shape. I've heard so many stories of note investors investing in a property without sending someone over to check on it, only to find out it was burnt down.

Don't let that be you.

Use wegolook.com/products/instant-inspections for that extra piece of mind. This service is awesome because they will take a picture of all 4 sides of the property. Sometimes, they can even take a few pictures of the inside if the windows don't have blinds. You can also make special requests if there is a particular point of interest.

THAT'S IT!

That's your team!

If you follow my advice and start out by brokering notes, you can get away with just hiring a realtor, a boots on the ground and a document custodian.

Now that we know who will be a part of your team once you find a note, it's time to learn about making sure your notes are worth your time!

6

DUE DILIGENCE

Residential note investing is a lot like residential investing. You still want to make sure the property you are investing in is in a city where someone will buy or rent it, is not surrounded by crime, and isn't too beat up. That said, there are still a few extra things you need to know, so try not to skip ahead, even if you think you know what you're doing.

Let's dive in!

WHERE TO INVEST

No matter how you advertise, you're going to get a lot of different notes in a lot of different cities. Afterall, a diverse portfolio is a safe portfolio! That said, you need to vet every city you seriously consider investing in.

There are 3 main criteria you should use to vet cities: crime, population, and unemployment. If the crime is too high, the population is too low, or the unemployment rate is too high, it could spell out problems for you. Do not fall into the trap of becoming a slumlord note investor - it usually ends in tears.

When it comes to where you should invest, note investing has two schools of thought. One of them is to choose your states and cities before you start investing. These note investors will only buy a note if it's in their previously vetted target investment zones. They choose their states before they start and stick to them almost without exception.

This strategy does limit where you can invest, but the upside is that you will know those areas very well and can quickly determine if your note is a deal or a dud.

The second strategy is to do cursory research on the city of any note that comes across your desk. The benefit is that you leave yourself wide open to invest in any note. The downside is that you won't have as much in-depth knowledge about the area you are investing in, which leaves you open to making more mistakes.

Lucky for you, the technique that I am about to show you will work for either of those processes.

Selecting your Ideal Cities

If you've decided to become an expert in a few cities around the US, then read on! The first step is to pick the cities. They should not be too rural, should not have a lot of crime, and should not have a high unemployment rate. Everything else is on the table!

It's time to make your first decision - are you going to invest in expensive mortgage notes or inexpensive mortgage notes? If you want to try for houses that are worth your time but not worth a lot of money, then you should stick to the midwest. And, of course, my recommendation is that you stick to these cheaper states to start with because it is much less risky to lose 20k than 200k. These midwestern states also tend to have less strict foreclosure laws. This works out in your favor because it takes less time to foreclose if your borrower stops paying.

However, if you have a lot of money laying around, then you might want to go with more expensive states. Those states are generally the states that touch an ocean. For some reason, the price of housing is constantly on the rise there.

Now that you've decided how expensive you want your notes to be, go look at a map and select a few states that you're interested in investing in. You don't need to know anything about the real estate in that state to invest there (yet) but it does help if you have a little background knowledge.

Pick one of the states you're interested in. Open up google maps and look at the major cities. Make a list of those major cities and their suburbs because these are the areas that we are going to start investing in!

Bestplaces.net is your Best Friend!

Whether you are doing preliminary research or you just had a note come across your desk and are interested in the surrounding area, the steps from here on out are the same. We are going to check on what I like to call The Big 3.

Go to bestplaces.net. Type in the town or zip code that you are interested in. A few statistics will pop up as well as some categories along the left side of the page. When we look at statistics, we want to look at them in the context of the overall country. We want whichever statistic we are looking at to beat the statistics for the United States.

In my opinion, the most important statistic is crime. If you have high crime in an area, that often means high unemployment rates and a greater potential for your investment to get broken into or burnt down.

So, let's start there.

If you look to the left, you'll see a "Categories" table. Open up the Crime tab. The top 2 sentences are pretty much all you need to know about that city. For instance, if I look at the 78754 zip code, I see the following picture.

Crime in Zip 78754 (Austin, TX)
Crime is ranked on a scale of 1 (low crime) to 100 (high crime)

Austin (zip 78754) violent crime is 32.2. (The US average is 22.7)
Austin (zip 78754) property crime is 60.2. (The US average is 35.4)

Austin Crime

As you can see, the violent crime and the property crime are very high compared to the US average. Does this mean this area is a bad place to invest?

Yes. It does.

You should move on unless you have a compelling reason to believe otherwise. If your town looks like that, then move on to another zipcode.

I moved on to a suburb right outside of Austin called Round Rock.

Crime in Zip 78665 (Round Rock, TX)
Crime is ranked on a scale of 1 (low crime) to 100 (high crime)

Round Rock (zip 78665) violent crime is 14.3. (The US average is 22.7)
Round Rock (zip 78665) property crime is 22.3. (The US average is 35.4)

Round Rock Crime

Ahh, much better. The violent crime and property crime are much lower than the US average which means this will be a safer place to invest.

Filtering this way is great because it will automatically get rid of a lot of the more risky investments in a portfolio. However, crime is just the first step of the big 3. The next one is the economy.

Move on to the economy tab. Similarly, when you open it up, you will see what you need for a cursory inspection of that area.

Economy in Zip 78665 (Round Rock, TX)

Round Rock (zip 78665) has an unemployment rate of 2.9%. The US average is 3.9%.

Round Rock (zip 78665) has seen the job market increase by 3.5% over the last year.
Future job growth over the next ten years is predicted to be 52.2%, which is higher than the US average of 33.5%.

Tax Rates for Round Rock (zip 78665)
- The Sales Tax Rate for Round Rock (zip 78665) is 8.3%. The US average is 7.3%.
- The Income Tax Rate for Round Rock (zip 78665) is 0.0%. The US average is 4.6%.
- Tax Rates can have a big impact when Comparing Cost of Living.

Income and Salaries for Round Rock (zip 78665)
- The average income of a Round Rock (zip 78665) resident is $32,011 a year. The US average is $28,555 a year.
- The Median household income of a Round Rock (zip 78665) resident is $85,048 a year. The US average is $53,482 a year.

Round Rock Economy

This part tells us a lot of very useful information. Some of it we need now and some we need later. Let's start at the top.

As you can see, the unemployment rate in Round Rock is 2.9% while the unemployment rate for the US is averaging at 3.9%. Both of those numbers are pretty low, but the fact that Round Rock beats the US means that it is likely experiencing a strong economy. Since there's low unemployment and a strong economy, it means that you don't need to worry about your borrower losing their job.

Let's move to the next line. The Job market. The job market has increased by 2.5% and is expecting to have a 52.2% increase over the next 10 years. That will beat the US growth rate by almost double!

Wow!

Our assumptions about the strong economy appear correct. And the growth rate can only mean that people will be flocking to Round Rock in droves over the next 10 years. That's great news for us because if we end up owning the house, we will be able to rent or sell it easily.

I've included the tax rates and the income and salaries in this screenshot as well. The tax is good to know for when you create your ROI calculator because if you end up foreclosing and owning the property, you will have to pay taxes on it.

As for the salaries, it's great to see if they make more than the national average, but you always want to take the extra time to check up on the cost of living. Click on the Compare

Cost of Living calculator. You should type in your potential investment town and another town (maybe your home town or another town you are interested in). Then, type in the US average cost of living. This will give you a pretty good indication of if this town has higher salaries because it's more expensive to live there or if it just has higher salaries because the job market is strong.

The last category of The Big 3 are the people stats. You use this tab to make sure people are actually moving into this city. Scroll down until you see the PEOPLE graph. About halfway down, you'll see a section for population.

Make sure the population is growing. If it's growing, that means people are moving in. This means that houses are likely to appreciate in this area and that it is overall a great place to start investing in mortgages because the mortgages were probably originated for less than the house is worth, so the borrowers are very unlikely to be underwater.

That's how you check a city to see if it's a great place to invest. If you are looking at cities preemptively, then do this for 100-200 of them. Don't cheat this step! It's really important to know what you're investing in before you invest in it.

Once you have 10-20 key cities, you should read up on that market and take notes. Join the REIA club on meetup and read the forums. Make sure you know everything you should know about that city.

If you come across a tape with properties outside of your key investment cities, then you can either perform this sniff test or you can pass on them. Either way, you'll turn a profit!

Before we move on, I want to give you a word of warning: be careful when you choose to invest in new markets. Each market is very different and has different problems.

Such as snow. It snows in some areas. What does this mean for your roof? Your pipes? What kind of A/C or heating does this area have? How old are the houses?

What are the foreclosure laws? Is it judicial foreclosure? What are the tax laws? Is it a redemption state?

All of these questions (and millions more) are drastically different for different parts of the US. Some areas might have problems you can't even think of on your own. (Like Termites, Tornados, Hurricanes, etc).

If you're purchasing notes all over the United States as a new investor, it leaves a lot of room for error. If you limit yourself to just a few areas, then you'll probably make all your major mistakes on your first few notes.

Trust me, no matter how much you read or prepare, you will make a mistake or two.

Luckily, these mistakes usually won't make or break your business, but they can be costly. I always think of my friend Tim when I decide to invest in new markets.

A few years ago, my friend decided that he was going to invest in a flip in Austin, Texas. Now, this guy was very green and had barely invested before, but he saw an opportunity and wanted to explore his options. The property in question had been on the market for over 180 days, was absolutely full of trash, and by all his calculations was an absolute steal.

So, after doing some due diligence, he decided to buy it. The title seemed good, the owners wanted to sell it, and the price was great. He thought he was going to make a killing on it by building a multifamily on the lot.

There was just one problem…

It had a gigantic tree right in the middle of the lot.

Obviously, he realized there was a tree there when he bought it. What he didn't know is that it's almost impossible to cut down this type of tree in the city of Austin.

That's right, it turns out Austin has a law restricting you from cutting down certain trees of a certain circumference. There are also laws about how close you can build a house to said trees.

He did eventually get the tree chopped down, but it took $20,000 and 12 months.

The more you spread out your investments, the more you open yourself up to mistakes.

If you stay within a state (or better yet, a city), then you will know the tax structure, tax sale rules, and the foreclosure time frames. You don't necessarily have to worry about tree laws when you invest in notes, but the taxes and foreclosures can turn a highly profitable deal into a dud in no time.

Another tip is to make sure you stick to the same type of property.

Whether that's owner occupied, rented out, or vacant. The strategy that you should follow for each is different.

Vacant homes are almost always foreclosures, owner occupied will usually be a workout or a cash for keys and a rented out house is usually a toss up. They all involve different strategies because investors, home owners, and vacant home owners all have different mindsets.

Hopefully you get the point, but to sum up this section, try to stay within the same general area when you invest. Invest in the same types of properties in the same states with the same team.

Anything outside of your core cities should be brokered to

another investor or passed up unless you do extensive research.

A NOTE AT LAST!

Picture this: You've been calling banks and posting on LinkedIn for a month now. You've had a few executives tell you they want to chat, but it hasn't really led to anything yet. It's noon on a Tuesday and you decide to eat some lunch.

Your phone rings.

It's a number you don't recognize so you suspect it is a spammer. Against your instincts, you pick it up anyway.

Thank god you picked up because it's a banker! He's calling you because he wants to see if you can help him offload some of his non-performing notes.

You had half expected to never receive a call from anyone who actually had a note to sell you, so you are absolutely delighted! That delight soon turns to fright when you wonder... *Now what?*

If this call is from a bank executive, you probably don't need to do that much. Explain that you can help them, ask them what a fair price is for the tape and ask what the deadline is. Tell them where they can email the tape and make sure you get their contact information before you hang up. Usually they'll tell you it's some amount of money, like 33 cents (meaning 33 cents for every dollar owed). The rest of the information you need should be in the tape.

If this is a seller financed note, then you have a little more work to do. Remember how I told you individual sellers aren't as put together as banks?

Well, that's going to come into play now.

They likely only have one note. They probably don't have any of the information on that note in a format that is useful to you. So, you're going to need to get some more information from them. Luckily, you've read this book and you have the form you need (you can find it by typing in note.beauxblast.com in any browser).

While you're on the phone, you're going to do a little screening. You want to make sure it is actually a note. I've heard of some horror stories of random people calling and saying that they want you to take over their rent (?!).

So, ask them the below questions anytime you get a call from a non-bank entity. If they do have a note for sale and the note seems worthwhile, you should email the form from my bundle at note.beauxblast.com.

SELLER FINANCE/SINGLE NOTE INTAKE FORM

Question	Explanation
Are you the one receiving payments on the mortgage?	Sometimes, people will see your ad and think that they can sell you the mortgage they are paying. It doesn't really work like that. You need to talk to the person collecting the payments, not paying the payments.
What collateral secures this note?	It can be anything from an office building to a mobile home. Whatever it is, you need to know. Different note buyers look for different properties. Some people might also call you about different types of notes like cars, credit card debt, etc. You only want real estate notes. I'd say ditch mobile homes without land as well.
Are the payments current? If they are not, how far behind are they? Foreclosure?	You want to know if it's performing, reperforming or non-performing. You also need to know if they have already started the foreclosure process.
What was the sales price?	This will tell you the original price that this property was sold for. Different investors have different price points, so it's important you know what the price point is.
When was the property originally sold?	If it was recently sold, then this note is worth less because it has not been seasoned.
How much did the buyer put down?	You need to make sure this amount was over $0. If the buyer didn't put anything down, there's a really high chance that they are going to default on their loan. People who don't have money to buy usually don't have money to pay their mortgage. I'd say a safe bet is over 5% of the sales price.
What is the balance of the mortgage?	Different investors will want different loan to values(LTVs). Usually, notes over 80% LTV are harder to market and sell.
Which position is the lien? If it's not the first position, what is the mortgage on the first?	You will have to pay appropriately for each position. First positions are the most expensive, seconds are less expensive. Anything past second is difficult to find a buyer for and is probably not worth your time because they are going to be extremely discounted.

Is there a balloon? If so, when is it due?	You don't want to purchase a loan with an impending balloon payment. If they are going to pay the balloon in less than 1 year, you need to be very careful. Why wouldn't they just keep the loan and wait for the payout? Don't get greedy.
Why do you want to sell this note? How much cash do you need right now?	You need to understand why they want to sell it in order to determine 2 things. 1. Are they serious about this? Do they have a good reason to sell? If it sounds like they have a good reason, then they are probably legitimate. If they don't have a good reason, dig deeper. Sometimes people sell notes because they are broken beyond repair, do not get caught up in a bad note! 2. How much of a discount can you get out of them. Maybe they need money for their son's college tuition. Maybe they want to buy a car. Maybe they've found another investment that they're interested in. Perhaps you can buy a partial or work out a creative deal. You don't just need to buy the whole note! Maybe there's a happy medium.
Where is the property located?	Some of your investors will only invest in some states. Some states are harder to invest in than others. It's important to know where the property is located because that's going to help you determine if you have a buyer.

Some of your investors will only invest in some states. Some states are harder to invest in than others. It's important to know where the property is located because that's going to help you determine if you have a buyer.

If you are satisfied with their answers, then you need to collect more in depth information about the collateral, the borrower, and the type of loan. Get their contact information and then email them your broker intake form. Even if you don't plan on brokering the note, it still has all the information you, as an investor, needs.

Here is an explanation of the questions on the broker worksheet that is provided in my bundle.

Question	Explanation
What is the property's address?	You will need the full address in order to perform full due diligence on the property.
Is it owner occupied or a rental? If it's a rental, is it currently rented? How much are they renting it for?	If it's a rental and it's not currently rented, this could spell trouble for the payor of the note. Investors need income in order to pay their expenses.
Describe the property and the surrounding area in detail.	You will be looking at the property in more detail, but you want to see if they know the crime statistics, if the area has had population increases and if the neighborhood is falling apart. You will verify this information later.
1) Who is the lender for each of the mortgages? 2) Is it FHA, VA, Private, or Conventional? 3) What is the current balance and interest rate? 5) What is the monthly payment without taxes and insurance? 6) What are the taxes and insurance?	You will need to know about the first mortgage if you are investing in a second. You need to know if the first mortgage will default soon, the likelihood of the borrower paying it, and how long it will take to pay off.
When is the next payment due?	You will want to be able to tell your investor when they can expect to see payments.
How often has the payor been late? Is there a reason?	If they have a history of being late, it could mean that they will default in the future. It also means that there may be more potential for foreclosure or a workout.
What is the payor's employment? What's the employer's number and address?	If they're unemployed, it's bad news. If they have seasonal employment, it could explain why they are consistently late. If they have a great job, then you know this mortgage will stay performing.
What's the payor's name, address, and Social. (They may not know the social).	Some investors perform a soft credit check before they invest. It's a highly debated topic.
What else should I know about the note, payor, property, or anything else?	Maybe they have some special circumstances. There might be some extra information.
What does the note holder think is a fair price?	Do not start negotiating, just take it in and let them know that you will see what you can do once you have performed due diligence. Asking them what they think is fair will probably cut down on the price a little as well.

Once they fill out and email you the form, you have all the information you need to perform your due diligence. It doesn't matter if you plan on brokering the note or investing in it yourself, you need to do the first round of due diligence. However, you only need to do the 2nd round if you plan on investing in it yourself.

I would suggest brokering the first 5 or 10 notes to other note investors (as long as you aren't using aggregation sites or rebrokering already brokered notes). As I've said before, this is the best way to do it because other note investors will tell you if your due diligence was good or bad *for free*. They will likely perform their own due diligence before returning with a yes or no. If it's a no, be sure to ask them why so you know what you need to add to your next round of due diligence.

One more note on brokering notes: make sure you have some end buyers before you start advertising your services. Some facebook note investing groups will have resources that tell you what the individual investors are looking for. You can also google "Note investors" to see some of the larger note investor's websites.

You can also purchase a list of note investors here: https://papersourceonline.com/registry-of-investors/how-to-get-it/ for $79. This list includes an explanation of what each note investor is looking for and a year's subscription to a newsletter all about note investing. Give it a shot - it's worth it.

Afterall, you need someone to buy the notes you're trying to broker. Or else, what's the point?

ROI CALCULATOR

A Return on Investment (lovingly referred to as ROI) calculator is exactly what it sounds like. It's an excel spreadsheet that tells you exactly what you're going to spend and make from a deal. It includes all the costs of due diligence, all holding costs, and all of the costs of business, like paying your team. It should also include the yield from different exit strategies so you can make an informed decision on which ones you would like to pursue and which ones are not profitable.

The remainder of the chapter will tell you what you need to know when building an ROI calculator and how to perform due diligence. Building your own ROI note investing calculator is a right of passage. Not only is it part of the learning process (You're going to learn so much more if you build your own.) it is surprisingly far less confusing.

Using another investor's ROI calculator is extremely confusing because you likely don't understand how it works. Very few people will give away their ROI calculator because they are so personalized. Even a simple one would probably end up doing more harm than good because you won't understand how to use it.

Luckily, this book gives you all of the information you need to build one for yourself.

Make sure you have Excel open as you go through the next 3 chapters because they all have due diligence, funding, and exit strategy information that you need for your ROI calculator.

DUE DILIGENCE ROUND 1 - CURSORY

Now that you have the address and some pricing information, you can start to perform due diligence. Whether the information is in your intake form or a spreadsheet from the bank - you should have everything you need to make a solid decision on whether to invest or not.

These first few rounds of due diligence are all about figuring out if the actual property is in a good area, has an ltv below 80%, and is in good shape. The cursory due diligence in round 1 is more about deciding if the house would be a good investment for you to purchase. If it seems like it's a solid house, then we are going to move on to deciding if the note is worth buying (which is covered in Due Diligence Round 2 and Chapter 7). As you go through these next few chapters, you should build your ROI calculator and bookmark all of the websites mentioned.

The first thing you want to start with is determining the value of the home. I always use the average of a few different websites because none of them are quite right. Open Zillow.com, eppraisal.com, and trulia.com.

Look up the address of the house on each of these websites. Now, gather the following information - current price, bedrooms, bathrooms, and square feet. Make sure they all match up on each website. If they don't, then make a note of it.

This is where knowing your market comes in handy. All of these websites will be wrong about the price - but you have no idea how wrong unless you have a firm grasp on the market. This will come in time, but for now, we're just going to do our best to approximate the value.

To calculate an approximate value for the home, take the average sale value that you get from those 3 websites and multiply it by 0.9. Keep in mind that this is a worst case, cursory value. If this property passes this round of due diligence, we're going to ask our realtor to give us his opinion. This is called a broker price opinion(BPO). If you're brokering this note, then a ballpark is good enough.

Next, we want to discover what the average days on the

market is. It's easy to find the days on market and the average listing price with realtor.com's market-trends analyzer tool. Go to https://www.realtor.com/research/market-trends/ and search for the state your property is in. Then, scroll down to the bottom. There should be a heatmap that will show information by metro area. Make sure you write down the days on market because this is likely how long you're going to need to hold this house if you end up owning it and want to sell it.

The next step is to look at the condition of the home. You should have seen some pictures on zillow, trulia, and eppraisal. You should also search for the property on google maps and google earth. Try to find the most recent pictures from those sites. It's simple on zillow/trulia, but it is a little less obvious on google street view so I'll attempt to give you some instructions.

On google Street view, if you look in the top left, there's a black box. In that box, there's a clock icon. Click on the clock. A new screen should appear and you will be able to see when the picture was last taken in the box in the top left. You should also search the address in youtube to see if there were any recent walkthroughs of the property or properties nearby.

If the pictures are recent and it doesn't look like the property is in a state of disrepair, we can move on to crime. Earlier, we looked at crime for an entire city, now we are going to check the direct area around the property. Every city has crime and we want to make sure we aren't investing in a pocket of crime. Why wouldn't you do this? It only takes an extra minute and it could help you avoid a high crime area in a low crime city.

We'll use Trulia for this. Go back to your trulia tab and look at the crime heat map. The area around the property should be mostly green. I like Trulia because it even shows you which crimes took place. If there is crime and most of it is petty crime, you're in the clear. If the area had major crime like murder then you should probably stay away from this one. It would be hard to rent to good renters, harder to sell, and there's a much higher chance that the borrower would just default again if you did a workout with them.

Speaking of rentals - one of the exit strategies is to rent the house. I like to use rentometer.com and zillow to estimate what I could get if I have to rent it out. Look up your property on each of these sites and then take the average of the rental values. It won't be perfect, but it will get you close.

The final step of our initial due diligence is to see if there is a tax lien against the property. We can find this out either by calling the county and inquiring or using the county's website. If the county has a website, you can find it on Netronline.com.

Once you are on netronline.com, you should see a list of counties. Click the county in question. This will bring you to their website. Every county website is different, so I can't tell you how to navigate it. Usually, if you look around for a little while, you will find a page that says "Property Search", "Appraisal", or something similar. When you find it, there will be a search bar that prompts you for the address. Once you find the property, you can see if any taxes are delinquent. If there are, make a note.

If you got a tape of properties and you found some that didn't quite meet your criteria, these are the properties that you will broker. For all of the notes that you're brokering, stop here. This is all the information you need to sell it to another investor. However, if you are planning on investing in a property, move on to Round 2 for more in depth analysis.

DUE DILIGENCE ROUND 2 - DEEP DIVE

Once you have separated the studs from the duds, it's time to really get to work! You want to make sure you only do this for properties you are 100% interested in because this step will cost you money.

We'll start by calling the county tax office. Earlier, we looked online to see if the borrower owes any taxes. Now, we want to call the county to make sure that the website was telling the truth.

When you are connected with the county clerk, ask them if this property has been through a tax sale within the last 4 years and if the borrower owes any taxes. If they have been through a tax sale, ask if they are still within the redemption period (If your state is a redemption state). You should know if it is a redemption state from your in depth city analysis earlier.

Redemption is a law that allows the original owner of the property xx months to reclaim their property if it was sold in a tax sale. Why would you ever buy a property in a redemption state? Because if the original owner decided that they wanted their property back, they would have to pay you the price from the auction + any fees you had to pay + interest.

Each state has a law that determines what the maximum interest rate you can charge is (some of them up to 22%!) so you can actually make a lot of money on tax sales in redemption states. However, you usually have to wait until after the redemption period to do anything to the property - so you're going to have to hold it for a while before you can sell it.

The next question is if there are any liens on the property. You will get an exact record of the liens and how much is owed on them later when you perform a title search. For now, it's good to know if there are liens.

The next step is to search pacer.gov for the borrower's records. Pacer.gov is the U.S. government's criminal and civil case repository. Any American can sign up in about 10 minutes. Attorneys and even reporters use this website all the time. We are going to use it to look at bankruptcy information on our borrowers.

Pacer.gov isn't free, but it is very cheap - less than $3 per case. Don't skip this step! 3 bucks is a small price to pay for this information.

We want to know if they've ever filed bankruptcy or if they are currently going through bankruptcy. If they are, it could mean trouble!

There are two types of bankruptcy: chapter 13 and chapter 7. Chapter 13 will create a court mandated payment plan while chapter 7 discharges the borrower of past debt. The debt is still attached to the property in chapter 7, but the borrower does not legally need to pay it back.

If they have filed a chapter 7, you're probably going to foreclose. If the borrower has gone through a chapter 13… you'll probably foreclose. The courts rarely make a payment plan the borrower can stick to. So, if they've already gone through bankruptcy, likely they will fail to pay back what they owed.

If it's an npn note, then it doesn't really matter. If it's a performing note, a bankruptcy on their record will devalue it.

Once you've determined they have not filed for bankruptcy, you should check their social media. Do not try to contact the borrower in any way because contacting them is illegal. Only use their social media to determine if they are going through major life changes, have a job, and spend their money wisely.

Honestly, you can probably skip this step if you have a whole stack of notes to look through, but it certainly won't hurt to know who you are doing business with. The previous seller might be dumping their note on you because their performing borrower called to say they can't pay.

The first step is finding the name of the borrower if you don't know it already. You should have been able to see it on the county tax records or from the intake form, but just in case you still need it, you can do a reverse search using the address on whitepages.com. Someone's name and phone number will come up. If you want, you can purchase the paid subscription because it will also give you criminal history and other information, but that isn't necessary.

Now that you have their name and phone number, you can easily search for them on social media. If it's public, their FaceBook will tell you if they are going through major life events. Maybe they were just fired, their spouse died, or they are going through some other life event. You don't know why they stopped paying. If you can figure out why, it will give you extra insight into which type of exit strategy you might need to take.

Can you do a workout?

Maybe you want to offer cash for keys?

Perhaps foreclosure is likely.

More on those in the next chapter.

Next, check LinkedIn to see what their profession is. Are they a professional? Are they a seasonal worker? Are they laid off? Again, all good information for deciding which exit strategy you are likely to take and if the seller was telling you the truth about why they are getting rid of this note.

If all of the above checks out, we'll move on to verifying the asset.

Long story short, you will need to get someone out there to take pictures and look at the house. One option is to ask your realtor to do it. Depending on how busy they are and what you promised them, they might be willing to give you a BPO.

Do not lie to the realtor, you don't want to get blacklisted from their town or their network. You want to be 100% honest with them about who you are and what you're trying to do. They may charge you $50 to $150 to look at your house and give you a BPO or they may do it for free. It just depends on the realtor and how good you are at negotiating.

A BPO is going to give you a fairly accurate picture of how much the property is worth. You should replace the purchase price you got earlier with this BPO. Make a note on how far off you were so you know for next time.

Ask the realtor if they are willing to take pictures of all 4 sides. If they aren't, then you should consider hiring the company https://wegolook.com/products/instant-inspections to take them. No matter who takes your pictures, make sure you ask them to pay attention to the following:

- Roof: Is there a blue tarp? Can they see shingles coming off? Does it look old and faded?
- Lawn: Is the grass overgrown or dead? Do the plants look well taken care of? Are there lights or decorations?

- Windows: Are the windows cracked or missing? Are the windows boarded up?
- Cracks in the foundation: Do they see any noticeable cracks in the foundation? Are there huge cracks on any of the exterior walls?
- Paint job: does the paint look like the neighbor's paint or is it more faded?
- Does the house look like the rest of the neighborhood in general or is it in worse condition?
- How does the fence look?
- Are there any huge holes in any of the walls, especially near to the ground?
- Are there water marks on the house?
- Are any of the doors or windows open?
- Can they see into any of the windows? Does the interior look well taken care of?

There's only so much you can tell from the exterior of the home. Since you don't own the property, there's no legal way to look at the interior unless you can see it through a window.

Vacant homes are usually less taken care of and have a greater potential for squatters. Very few squatters have "pride of ownership". Usually they destroy the house - holes in the walls, filth on the floor, needles... Be very careful with vacant houses. You will probably still have to go through an eviction process to get rid of squatters.

Before you get off the phone, ask your realtor what the average price for water, sewage, electricity, and gas are. You need an estimate of holding costs in case you take possession of the property. Make sure you also ask what percentage realtors in the area charge to sell a home and include that in your selling costs. If you do sell the house, make sure you work with that realtor. They helped you out on the front end, so you need to live up to your word and help them on the backend.

The last step is to figure out what your retainer fees and other costs will be. When we made our team, we found an attorney, a servicing company, a title company, a document custodian, and a property manager. It's time to call all of these companies and ask what their prices are.

For attorneys, you need to ask what their retainer fee is, what the cost to pull and examine title is, and what the average cost for foreclosure in the area is. Make sure you factor all of this into your profit margin.

For the servicer, you need to ask what their monthly retainer fee is, what services they offer, and what their processes are.

For the title company, ask how much they charge for pulling

title and what the general fees for closing are. You might consider using them instead of the attorney if they are cheaper. You can also pit their prices against https://www.protitleusa.com/, a website that does title searches for real estate investors.

I don't recommend you get a title search until later on in the process, like when you're closer to closing. If you want to be very cautious, you could pay for the 2 owner report from Protitle now. It costs $75.

For the document custodian - you need to know what their price structure is and how their process works.

For the property manager, you want to know what their price structure is and if they have any rehab companies that they recommend. If you come in possession of the home, you may need to repair it.

You can also ask them about the area you are investing in to see what average rents are and if it is a good area for investing. Like realtors, they know the area and can give you some great insight.

The more you know about the area, the better.

7

THE 9 MOST SUCCESSFUL EXIT STRATEGIES (IN ORDER OF PROFITABILITY)

Now that you have successfully obtained a note... what now? Let's talk about how you are going to make money.

Brokering notes has been covered at length throughout this book. In fact, it's one of the exit strategies! You know how to do due diligence, find investors, and fill out the investor intake form. Once you find another investor that wants to buy your deal, voila! You're pretty much done. All you have to do at that point is talk to your lawyer, your title company, and your document custodian.

Yes, brokering notes is a great exit strategy. You're going to broker notes throughout your investment career, so it is definitely a strategy you need to understand.

The problem that most note investors run into with

brokering is that it's a short term strategy. It gives you a lump sum for your trouble, but it does not give you long term income. This chapter is about the other 8 exit strategies you use when you would like to generate some income.

As a note investor, you can choose to invest in performing or non-performing notes. When you purchase a performing note, your next step is to either sell the note or hold the note. On the flip side, the goal for a non-performing note is to get it performing again and season it. Then you can sell it.

When you take possession of a non-performing note, the first thing you should ask your attorney to do is send a letter of foreclosure.

It feels nasty but it does its job. Lots of people think if they don't acknowledge their bank's warnings, the bank can't take their house away. A foreclosure usually wakes people up. Besides, even if you have every intention of working with the borrower, sometimes you can't avoid foreclosure. It's better to start on it early because it can take a year or more to process.

It's one of those "Better to have it and not need it than need it and not have it" situations.

You can stop the foreclosure process at any time, so all you're doing is spending a little extra money to let your borrower know you're serious and that they need to discuss their options… or else.

Once your foreclosure letter is sent out, you should start trying to contact the borrower. Your servicer will do this for you and make sure that you are compliant with all laws. If you can get in touch with them, your goal should be to find a loan modification that works for both parties. A loan mod works if you make money and they can pay their mortgage.

If, for some reason, they can't do a loan mod then the next best thing is cash for keys or a short sale. Sometimes, people have their head in the sand and don't want to come to terms with the fact that they are losing their house. They insist that you can't take their house and refuse to sell it.

It's heartbreaking when that happens, but it does happen. Unfortunately, when borrowers won't work with you, they leave you no choice but to foreclose. You'll be thankful that you took my advice and started foreclosing early when you discover that you have purchased a note attached to an unreasonable borrower.

After you are done reading this chapter, you'll have a clear idea on the steps you should take when talking with your npn borrowers. Make sure you add a yield column in your ROI calculator for each of the strategies I mention later.

That way, you can decide which one you want to go through with for each note.

If you invest in non-performing notes, there's one more thing we need to talk about before we talk about structuring your deal... which is how to talk to the borrower so that a deal can happen! Some borrowers are more than willing to work with you. Others will ignore all your calls. Still others will answer your calls and make you wish you ignored them.

I figured it would be nice to include a few tips on talking to your borrowers. The way you approach them makes a difference because if they don't like you, they are not going to try to work with you. This way, even if you hire it out (which you should!) you'll be able to tell if your servicer is doing a good or bad job.

TALKING TO THE BORROWER

The borrower is going through the worst crisis in their life right now. Yes, that crisis involves losing their house but often includes some other tragic event. When you speak with them, think of them like you would speak with someone you love.

Sometimes, the borrower will be rude to you or hang up. Do not let these interactions cause you to treat them unprofessionally - always treat them with dignity and respect.

Remember, this is your business. You need to be professional, cordial, and respectful every time you speak with them.

When you get a hold of them, your goal is to build rapport and figure out what their situation is. One of the ways you do that is by asking questions and listening to the answers. You should ask a lot of questions because every situation is different and the more you make people talk about themselves, the more they like you.

That said, you really just need the answers to these two questions...

First, **what happened that caused them to stop paying**? Sometimes, if you can just figure out what their problem is you can find an easy solution that works for everyone.

Second, **what do they want to do about the loan**? Get their feedback. Are they willing to modify the loan? Are they willing to sell their house?

Do not interrupt the borrower when they are answering your questions. A lot of them have a long story and will ramble. Let them talk and be sure to actively listen. Your borrower will be more willing to work with you if they feel like you hear them and are on their side.

Once you have the answers you need, you should ask them about their finances. What is their current income and what are their expenses. Can they afford to pay arrears AND the current monthly payment? If not, what can they pay? Does it fit in with what you need to charge to be profitable yourself?

The best case scenario is finding a loan modification that works for them and is profitable for you. Loan mods are fast and the quickest way to start collecting payments. All of the other methods are fine, but they will take longer.

Keep in mind that the quicker the borrower starts making payments, the faster you start seasoning your loan. If your plan is to flip these notes, then you want to start the seasoning process as quickly as possible.

With that in mind, let's talk about your exit options.

LOAN MODIFICATION

Loan mods are also known as workouts and they are the happiest ending for a non-performing note. It's the quickest, easiest and usually cheapest way to turn a npn into a performing note. It's also a very compassionate way to turn a profit.

A lot of the properties that need loan mods are underwater - meaning the borrowers owe more on their loan than their home is worth. Usually these borrowers bought their property at the top of the market back in 2007 and haven't been able to pay it down. Being underwater prevents the borrowers from refinancing or selling the home, so really their only choice is to keep paying the mortgage or let it go to foreclosure.

Sometimes, misfortune can also cause the borrower to stop paying. Maybe they got sick, their spouse died, or they lost their job. There are a variety of reasons that are all extremely sad. If you do end up calling and speaking with your borrowers instead of paying a servicing company, you will hear about some absolutely heartbreaking situations and be more than happy to help. Lots of good people get lost in the system - you can be the light that helps them find their way out. Just because borrowers are behind on their payment does not mean they are bad people. Sometimes, bad things happen to good people. Always assume they are good people unless you are given reason to think otherwise.

The determining factor for profit on these notes is the unpaid loan balance (UPB). You want to buy these notes for less than 50% of the UPB. That means if the house is worth $100,000, but the UPB is $70,000, you want to try to buy the note for $35,000.

The formula for this calculation is:

UPB x .5 = Maximum purchase price.

So, substituting in the numbers from earlier...

$70,000 x .5 = $35,000

If the property is underwater, you should aim for lower than 50%. You need to pay less than the house is worth because you might own it.

Similarly, if the situation is temporary - like a lost job - you can try to put them on a forbearance plan. This is basically a temporary workout where they make no or reduced payments for an agreed upon period of time.

That said, before you set your heart on forbearance, try to figure out a way to help them.

If you can figure out what their financial situation is and why they aren't able to pay their mortgage, you might be able to help them. Maybe your borrower has a lot of extra debt they just can't seem to pay off. You might be able to lighten their load by adding it to their mortgage. This is one trick note investors use to help their borrowers.

Let's say they took out a personal loan for 18% interest and they just can't seem to pay it off. You, as the note holder, can pay it off and add it to their mortgage.

This does two things.

One, the borrower can catch up because they aren't paying an exorbitant interest rate.

Two, you now make more money on your loan because you absorbed their debt and are charging them a modest interest rate.

Something like this can really help your borrower get back on their feet. Just make sure the total price of the loan does not exceed the value of the home.

How high is too high?

Well, you should aim to never have a loan that is worth more than 70% of the home. Why? Because if worse comes to worse, you can sell it to an investor. Normally turnkey investors will pay up to 80% loan to value (LTV). That gives you a neat 10% profit.

This exit strategy is usually the first one note investors try to make work. It takes the least amount of time, it helps the most amount of people, and gives you some quick cash flow.

One caveat: this strategy only works if the borrower is willing to work with you. If they aren't even returning your calls, then you probably will not be able to modify their loan. I've heard stories of investors going through the entire foreclosure process only for their borrower to beg for help the day before the sale. By that point, it's too late because the investor has already paid all of the costs of foreclosure and a workout is no longer profitable.

Hopefully, the borrower is willing to work with you. Either way, there are situations in which a workout is impossible. Let's talk about the next best strategy - cash for keys.

CASH FOR KEYS

Cash for keys is exactly what it sounds like - you give your borrower some cash and they hand you their keys. It is also known as Deed in Lieu.

One major problem (for some note investors) with this exit strategy is it leaves you with the asset. That's why we factor in the cost of realtors and property managers. If you choose to sell your new property, you should factor in the realtor fees. Similarly, if you choose to rent your new property, you need to factor in the cost of a property manager.

This strategy works best when there are no liens on the home because they will still be attached after you take possession. If there are liens present, use your best judgement and include them in your ROI calculator.

There is no set formula to figure out what to offer the borrower when you try to offer them cash for keys. It's always a negotiation. This is part of why getting to know them earlier in the process was so important - the more you know, the easier it will be to determine how much money they need in order to accept your proposal.

That could mean paying for a month's worth of rent, paying for their moving costs, or just giving them some cash… it all depends on the borrower's situation. That's why finding out their situation is so important.

That said, normally it's not more than $5000, but use discretion and make sure it's still profitable.

If you've ever dealt with people who are losing their homes, you might be wondering how you can keep the borrower from destroying their property before they go. It's not really that common for someone to destroy a house - but it does happen. If you'd like to protect yourself from this, you should include a clause in your deed-in-lieu agreement that the home needs to be move-in ready or the borrower forfeits the cash.

Once you have agreed with the borrower that cash-for-keys is the way to go, pay for an inspection. If the property is in bad shape and needs flip level repairs, make sure the deal is still profitable to sell to a flipper (or flip it yourself, if you're so inclined).

Flippers will pay up to 70% after repair value (ARV) minus the expected cost of repairs. Make sure you know what the price would be if the house was fixed up, multiply that by 0.7 and then subtract the estimated total cost of repairs.

SHORT SALE/SALE

Of course, the borrower can always just sell their house. If they do that, then they will pay you whatever they had left on the note and be done with it.

But, what if they're underwater?

When the borrower is underwater but willing to sell, you can give them permission to sell their home for less than what is left on the mortgage note. This strategy is known as a short sale.

As you've probably guessed, there are some risks associated with rubber stamping a short sale. Most of the time, dishonest borrowers will use this strategy to buy time.

There are a few ways you can protect yourself from these one-off situations.

You could follow my advice and always start the foreclosure process immediately upon possession of the note. If the borrower can't sell their property by the foreclosure sale, then they get foreclosed on. Using my stick and carrot analogy, this would be the stick strategy.

The carrot is offering the borrower a certain percentage of whatever they sell the house for. A few thousand dollars can go a long way towards making a bad actor do what they should be doing.

There's one more thing that you need to watch out for if you're attempting a short sale - jr. liens. If the borrower has any other liens on the property, they need to be paid off before closing. If they can't do that, then you only have one option left...

FORECLOSURE

Foreclosure is a necessary evil that most people try to avoid. It's painful for the borrower because they're losing their home and it's painful for you because it's expensive, tedious, and can take more than a year.

You, as an investor, should at least grasp the basics of foreclosure in your state. Most of the responsibility of actually following laws and filling out paperwork will fall on your lawyer, but it's always good to know the basics yourself.

Here is a quick reference for each state's foreclosure laws: https://madisonmanagement.net/investors/foreclosure-by-state/.

If you looked at the above link, you probably have a few

questions. For instance, what is non Judicial vs Judicial and what does that mean for me? Should I just use the court costs and attorney fees from this chart instead of calling an attorney and asking what their fees are? Why doesn't this tell me how long it will take to go through the foreclosure process?

Let me try to answer some of your questions so you have a full understanding of foreclosure. First, I want to start out by saying you should always act as if a foreclosure will take a minimum of 12 months. It's a long process with a lot of back and forth, so you always want to consider the worst case scenario.

There are 2 types of foreclosure in the United States - Judicial and non-judicial. If it's non-judicial, it means the lender does not have to go through the courts system to foreclose. This can speed up the foreclosure process because you don't have to wait on a trial.

As you might have suspected, judicial foreclosures go through the state court system. That means that the courts are involved in every step of the process. If you happen to invest in a state that is extremely backlogged, it can cause the process to drag on even longer because you have to wait for a court date.

Some states also have extra laws to protect the borrower

from the bank. California, Colorado, Minnesota, and Nevada have homeowner protection laws that slow down foreclosure tremendously. There are also national laws in place that prevent you from starting the foreclosure process until the borrower is more than 120 days late on their payments.

Some of the fastest foreclosure states are Virginia, Montana, Alaska, Oregon, and Mississippi. If you are really worried about foreclosing, you could start in any of those states. However, I want to remind you that it is possible to invest in npns and only rarely foreclose upon your borrowers. Some note investors hardly ever foreclose because they are usually able to do a workout. On the flip side, some note investors love to foreclose. It depends on who you are and what you are trying to do.

If your aim is to own the property, then foreclosure might be something you do pretty often. My advice is to target vacant homes because the home owner probably isn't as emotionally invested.

I spoke with one vacant homeowner who was totally fine with foreclosure, did not want to try to sell and would not work anything out even though I explained that it would wreck his credit. He just wanted the problem gone. Hard to believe, but there are people like that out there.

Luckily for you, you don't need to know a whole lot about

foreclosure to start investing in notes. There's a lot to say about it - an entire series could be written on foreclosure - but your lawyer and servicing company will handle most of the heavy lifting. So you just need to know how much it will cost, how long it will take, and the basics of the foreclosure laws in your investment states. Your team will take care of the details.

When you add foreclosure to your ROI calculator, make sure you add 12 months of holding costs. If it's a vacant house, the holding costs usually include lawn or snow service, taxes and maybe utilities.

You should also pay someone to drive by your property every month and check if it has attracted any squatters. If there are, your first priority should be to call the police and make them leave. Some states have laws that make them legal tenants after a certain period of time.

If your asset is not vacant, your holding costs are probably just the cost of taxes. You need to pay these because if you don't, the property could be put up for a tax sale auction.

Now that we've gone through a couple scenarios for non-performing notes, we'll go through some exit strategies for performing notes and notes that you've taken possession of.

SELLING AND RENTING THE PROPERTY

If you find yourself in possession of a property, then you have a few choices. You could either sell the property or you could rent it. When you sell it, one of two things will happen. Either the buyers will buy the house through another bank or they will buy the house through you.

Different states have different laws, so make sure you speak with your attorney before you attempt to seller finance a note. Some states do not allow seller financing, some states require a license and other states only allow you to do a handful each year. You can find most of the information online, but it's always safer to ask a lawyer.

If you don't want to seller finance, the buyers can always go the traditional route and either pay cash or finance through a bank. Since you are selling the house, you get to determine what the price is - but don't forget that you are paying all holding costs while you wait. That can mean all amenities, lawn or snow maintenance, taxes and anything else that is typical in your investment state.

So, even though you could wait to get top dollar for your property, it's probably best to price it to sell. Most investors will price it at 80-90% of the total value of the home.

The other thing you can do is rent. This is why we found a

property manager for our team - it will be their responsibility to find a renter. You could try to rent the home out yourself, but it would probably be difficult and will take time away from more important business activities - i.e. finding notes.

Whichever route you choose to go, it will cost you money. You should have all this information from your calls earlier - so make sure you include it in your ROI calculator.

SELLING THE NOTE

Selling a note is a little different than selling a property. When you sell a note to another investor, you are selling them the debt. Your note should be seasoned for at least 1 year with 0 late payments if you want to get maximum returns. The same rules apply here as selling any other note - you sell it at a percentage of the UPB.

You can also sell a partial from the note. As we talked about earlier in chapter 3, you can sell partials of your note to make back some of your profit. All you need to do is find investors who are willing to make less yield than you.

For instance, if you're getting an 18% return, then find someone who will happily invest for 12%. If you need a refresher on this topic, visit chapter 3 and run through some of the problems again.

REFINANCING

You cannot change the interest rate or the terms of the note without the borrower's consent. You both signed a contract and you both have consequences for breaking it. However, you can work with your borrower to give them an even better rate so that it is advantageous for them to refinance.

For instance, you can forgive some of their debt, but raise their interest rate so they owe less but are still paying you the same amount. If you do this, it is in their best interest to take their business elsewhere and refinance because they will probably get a lower interest rate and thus pay less each month. Just make sure the amount they have left in their balance is still profitable for you! When they refinance, you get the entire balance on the note in the form of a lump sum.

Of course, you need to make sure the loan has been performing for at least 1 year. If they had bad history, then you need to make sure it has been performing for at least 2 years. Most institutions will allow a refinance if the note has been performing for 2 years with no missed payments, even after bad payment history.

HOLDING THE NOTE

Last but not least, you could hold the note for cashflow. This is definitely a popular strategy for those who want passive income from notes and it is the best way to increase your wealth long term. You won't have to work as hard to buy and sell notes if you keep a few for passive income. In fact, many people are happy to retire on 20 or 30 performing notes.

8. 10X YOUR PORTFOLIO

Now that you know what notes are and how to purchase them, I'm going to share how you can start your own note investing business. There are a few different ways to fund notes - but some of them are more risky and creative than others.

Like regular real estate investing, investing in notes has an advantage over the stock market because you can leverage your money. If you don't like the idea of leveraging your money, you certainly don't have to. However, it makes it easier to invest if you do.

YOUR OWN MONEY

While using your own money is the least risky strategy financially, you should weigh the risk with your opportunity cost. There's no problem starting with your own money, but you will quickly run out after you purchase a couple of notes - especially if you purchase performing notes.

The law of 72 that I mentioned earlier says that if you get an 18% return, you double your money every 4 years. That's really not bad and 18% returns are not out of the question for this investment model, but what if you could put even more money into notes?

If you only invest $1000, after 4 years, all you have is $2000. But, if you invest $50,000, then after 4 years, you have $100,000. Even if you have to pay your investors some of your return, you would still make more total money than you could by yourself.

OTHER PEOPLE'S MONEY(OPM)

If you are broke or the idea of leveraging OPM intrigues you, then there are a few ways that you can get more money. I'm going to list them from worst to best. OPM is the lifeblood of real estate. You want to start using OPM as soon as you can because it's the only way you're going to scale.

Hard Money

Hard money is not the best option for this business model. Hard money will often charge you 8%-18% depending on where you live. Let's take the middle of the road assumption that you will be making 18% on any given note.

If you use hard money, your profits will quickly disappear. If you manage to find a hard money lender offering a 10% interest rate with 2 points on the front end, you'll make a little more than a 6% yield (because of the 2 points on the front end). This isn't bad, especially for not putting up very much of your own money, but I know that you can do better.

You can find hard money investors by searching for them online or going to your local REI club. But, before you start trolling for them, let's read about a few more strategies.

Private Investors

Private investors are another tricky one. First, there are lots of laws around fundraising from private investors. You need to make sure that you are following all of them. Lots of people use private investors to fund their notes, so it isn't impossible… however, if you're just starting out, it's one more thing you need to spend time figuring out.

Secondly, you have to find them and figure out what they think a good investment looks like. Private investors can only be people that you know. Once you've found a few people you have a personal relationship with that would like to invest with you, you need to learn about what they think a good investment looks like. It doesn't matter if they've never invested before or if they've invested 100 times, everyone has an idea of what a good investment looks like.

It's best to collect business cards or contact information and call them when you have what you think is a good deal. Don't try to collect money before you have something concrete if this is your first deal. People are much easier to work with when they can see what they're investing in.

If this is your first deal, then show them your investment and explain how the investment works. After you've done a few deals, your private investors are not going to invest in a single note, they are going to invest in *you*. They can use your past performance to decide if they want to invest with you or not instead of looking at a single deal.

There are 4 things that most of these private investors look for: protecting their capital, realistic returns, your track record, and a long term relationship. Most private money lenders will only want to work with a few really profitable investors. It makes it easier and more passive for them because they know they have money coming in every month.

Private investors also want realistic returns. Usually this sits around 8%. They're willing to put their money into notes because they know notes are more stable than the stock market. If they've never heard of notes before or have never even considered investing, it will be up to you to convince them that notes are a great investment and you are the investor who will grow their wealth.

Once you do find a private investor, make sure you treat them fairly and professionally. The higher ROI you give them, the happier they will be. Happiness means they will continue to invest with you and might even give you more money to invest. An added bonus: they'll talk about their amazing returns with their friends! That's free advertising.

Private investors definitely have their place in note investing. New investors have a hard time finding private investors unless they already have a deal in hand. When you get more experience, you naturally find more private money because you have a proven track record.

So, private money will be important to you later on, however when you first start out, you're going to have to find a deal before anyone is willing to invest with you.

Partnering

Partnering is like free tuition. If you find a note and can't pay for it, do not give up! Find a partner.

When you look for a partner, try to find someone that has something you don't - namely experience, money, or connections. You could even offer to give them the note in exchange for the ability to shadow them throughout the process.

Your partner should either finance the deal, give you advice, or both. If they are experienced note investors, they'll let you know right off the bat if your note is worth their time. If they aren't experienced investing in notes, then it'll be up to you to convince them to partner with you. Partnering up works really well for new investors, so I would definitely recommend this one!

You can find partners in all the usual places - FaceBook groups, BiggerPockets, and REIA meetings.

Brokering Notes

If you have no money or are just starting out, brokering notes should be your main strategy. It is, by far, the best way to invest in notes.

We've talked about this at length through the book, but I am going to summarize how it works for you here anyway.

Let's say you called a bank and they gave you a tape of 10 notes that has UPB of $100,000. The seller wants to sell his tape for 33 cents. Now that you have an actual deal, you perform some basic due diligence and then get to work!

You call all of the investors that you've collected contact

information from and tell them about the tape or the individual notes they might be interested in. If you end up selling one of the notes for 35 cents, that means the extra 2 cents is yours! Remember, that's actually $2000. It's out of $100,000, so 2 cents on the dollar is $2000.

After you find all of those investors, it's time to set up a double close. A double close is when you close with the buyer and the seller on the same day in different rooms. You don't want the buyer and the seller to see each other because they might cut you out when a new deal comes around! Your attorney and title company will know exactly how to set this up, so all you have to do is mention it.

Let's say you later find an even bigger portfolio worth even more notes. Instead of 2 cents, you take possession of one of the notes and use the spread to pay for it. Both of these strategies are common among new and old investors alike. Lots of times you'll come across a tape and only keep the good notes. There's nothing wrong with shopping around the deals that don't quite meet your criteria.

Business Lines of Credit

You can apply for a business line of credit through whichever business entity you have for your note business (Most people do LLCs).

I believe this is the best loan to use for investing in notes. If you have an excellent credit score, you could have interest rates as low as 3%. Imagine only being charged 3% on an investment that would make you 12%. That's an insane spread!

When you are a new business owner, banks often base the terms of your Business Line of Credit on your own personal credit score. So, if you have bad personal credit, they will likely pass on your application.

However, if you can get one, you have a huge advantage. Business lines of credit are like an unholy marriage between credit cards and bank accounts. They are like bank accounts because you have full use of the "cash" in your account up to the limit. They are like credit cards because you often only have to pay interest on what you owe. So, if you leave your business line of credit open with no charges, you don't pay anything to keep it open. But you can use it like cash if an investment comes around.

If you have a high enough credit score and manage to keep a good relationship with your bank, business lines of credit are an excellent way for people just starting out to get more money.

CONCLUSION

Wow! You made it!

Thanks for sticking with me and reading the entire book. I hope that you at least found one new idea in this book and have the confidence to start investing in notes today. There was a lot to learn and I tried to distill it into a few concise chapters for you.

We talked about what notes are and how we can use them. You also learned a lot of the vocabulary and were challenged to think about how much risk you can handle to figure out what kind of note you want to invest in.

If nothing else, I hope you come away from this book with the confidence to get started. Nothing ever happens if you don't take action. I do not expect this book alone to make you proficient in note investing - you'll have to read more, look at more videos and make a lot of friends. My goal was to give you a head start on note investing - I want you to go into this business with your eyes wide open!

Now that you know all that stuff, what's the plan? If I had to make a checklist, it would look something like this:

1. Decide which type of note and which states you want to invest in
2. If you have some money, use one of the note aggregation sites to purchase a performing note. Get a feel for how the process goes and who the major players are.
3. Start advertising! Pick one or two advertising methods and go for it. Stick with those methods for at least 6 months.
4. When you find a deal, assemble your team and broker the deal! There isn't really a magic number of deals you should broker before you're ready to start investing on your own, it could be 1 or it could be 10. Just broker a few so you get a feel for what notes are worth and how to do due diligence.
5. After you've brokered a few, keep a per npns and try to work through them.

Does that look over simplified to you? Good! The process is actually very simple. Find notes, sell some notes, keep some notes… Once you wrap your head around that, it will make investing easier for you. Lots of new investors find notes every day and you can too! You just have to stick with it.

Thank you so much for being a part of my journey. I am so glad that I get to be a part of yours. If you liked this book or even learned one new thing, please leave a 5 star review! It really helps my business and gets the word out about different investing strategies people can use to reach their own financial freedom.

Until Next Time!

Beaux

NOTE INVESTMENT CHECKLIST

(NEVER LEAVE HOME WITHOUT THIS...)

This Checklist will...

- Help you determine if a note is worth your time in 5 minutes
- Be the ONLY Note Intake form you will EVER need
- Is designed to share with other investors for quick turnaround
- **BONUS Checklist: Common Documents needed to assign OR close**!

The last thing we want is for you to get caught with your pants down when someone calls you with a deal. Download this checklist so you always know what to say when a potential lead calls!

To receive your Note Investing Checklist, visit the link:

www.BeauxBlast.com/Debt

REFERENCES

- Biggerpockets.com
- Paperstac.com
- Notesdirect.com
- https://www.watermarkexchange.com/
- https://www.bankbranchlocator.com/banks-in-usa.html.
- https://www.creditunionsonline.com/search_usa.html
- Listsource.com
- Click2mail.com
- Reiskip.com
- 10bii Calculator - The Calculator that calculates interest. You can get a physical calculator or download the app.
- rule of 72

- LegalLeague100.com
- https://www.distressedpro.com/special-servicers-list
- https://wegolook.com/products/instant-inspections
- bestplaces.net
- https://www.realtor.com/research/market-trends/
- Zillow.com
- Truilia.com
- Eppraisal.com
- Rentometer.com
- Netronline.com
- Pacer.gov
- Whitepages.com
- https://wegolook.com/products/instant-inspections
- https://www.protitleusa.com/
- https://madisonmanagement.net/investors/foreclosure-by-state/.

Made in the USA
Columbia, SC
24 July 2023

986663c5-ac85-4cbe-b3e7-6ecbe3f295ccR02